The Marriage Coaches

I Love Being Married

A Guide to Divorceproof Your Marriage

Benjamin Walker, Jr. & Alisha Curry Walker, MS, LPC

Straight A Publishing Group

I Love Being Married: A Guide to Divorceproof Your Marriage

Copyright © 2013 Benjamin Walker, Jr. & Alisha Curry Walker

Requests for information should be addressed to:

The Marriage Coaches, 2045 Mt. Zion Rd. Suite 311 Morrow, GA 30260

ISBN-10: 0615744443

ISBN-13: 978-0615744445

All Scripture used unless otherwise noted are from The Holy Bible, New King James Version

This book is meant as a resource and support to help you repair, restore and revitalize your marriage. In no way is this book meant to replace the use of professional help if needed.

Cover design by Chrissi Major

Edited by Nicole Lester

Printed in the United States of America

DEDICATION

This book is dedicated to God and our children, Brandon, Alexis
Allana, Aaliyah and Angelique

CONTENTS

ACKNOWLEDGEMENTS

We thank God for planting the vision for us to bring forward the I Love Being Married Movement. Only you know the sleepless nights, the work and effort it took to bring this book together. Thank you for pruning us both and making us a better couple in the process.

Brandon, Alexis, Allana, Aaliyah and Angelique the best children in the world. Daddy and Mommy thank you for your support of us finishing this book and being patient while this last baby (book) is born. You all have inspired us to move forward with this book even when we didn't want to, so that we could leave a legacy for you. We especially thank Liquee for showing us how to push through by her example of living every day. We love you all.

First , we would like to give great THANKS to our Lord and Savior Jesus Christ who has given my wife and I this opportunity to share with you what he shared with us many years ago. There have been so many challenges, situations, circumstances, triumphs and trials that have brought us to this point. My beautiful wife and I would like to take this time to thank ALL of the special people who have blessed us with their kind words, wisdom, love, words of encouragement and inspiration.

Benjamin Walker, Sr., thank you for your love and guidance, but most importantly thank you for modeling for me what a REAL man/father looks like. You taught me early on how to love myself then, you taught me how to take care of me. It was like yesterday I can still hear you saying, "Are you watching me, are you paying attention because one day you will have to teach these same things to your own children". Daddy you are my

HERO, I am proud to say that you are the reason that I am the man that I am today. I love you daddy.

Evelyn M. Marion my mother, the one who labored with me in her womb for 10 months, I thank you for giving birth to me, I thank God for you. You have been my motivator when I wasn't sure if I could do it, you taught me to travel the road less traveled and to take chances because we only live once. You loved me with accountability. However, the thing that resonates with me the most is you are not just my mother you are my sister in Christ, a place we both share with God that I cherish dearly. I love you mommy

Thomas and Gwendolyn Curry, the best parents any girl could ask for. You have shown me what true unconditional love really looks like and we really do appreciate all that you have done to support us and our family.

Twandolyn Walker, the big sister who gave me a hard way to go growing up, but LOVED me and protected me, thank you for your protection. Love you Captain Walker

Nicole Stoakley , my little sister who jumped the broom 5 years before I did and showed your older brother how it was supposed to be done. Thank You for being that example. I love you baby girl.

Adriane Curry Simpson, thank you for always supporting me and my marriage even from the start on the wedding day. Thanks for being a great auntie to the girls and now bringing in their uncle.

J'on Simpson, thank you for coming into our family and blending so well. Thank you for loving my sister and loving our girls the way you do. Thank you to our new extended family, the Simpsons and the love they have shown us and their support of the girls.

Rev. Michael Cousin we thank you for being the first person to see our vision almost 14 years ago and helped us by allowing us to interview strong couples on a Sunday morning service. Under your ministry, our love for married couples was born.

Rev. Dr. Craig L. Oliver, Sr. and Rev Henderson, thank you for allowing us to become a part of such a vibrant marriage ministry and allowing us to help other couples prepare for marriage. We thank Pastor Oliver for his leadership and commitment to growing men.

Rev. Eddy and Mrs. Roberta Moise, we thank you for being our accountability partners, our sounding board and our ear when we need support for our marriage and our family. Thank you for your love for us and your friendship.

Rev. Milton Campbell we thank you for your prayers and support. You have been a great guide in our journey to fulfilling God's call on our lives and we really do appreciate you and your wife Christina.

Helen and Harvey Brown we thank you for your support and prayers for our work and the completion of this book.

Walter and Dr. Brenda Snipes thank you for being like second parents to me and supporting my family.

Frank and Juanita McClellan thank you for your love support and continues prayers for our family.

Lewis and Rev. Earline Brown thank you for being like a second mom and dad to me and for loving and supporting my family.

To our loving and supportive aunts and uncles, who show us unconditional love, Liz, Diane, L.C., Sam, Carolyn, Chris, Louise, Alice, and Luther.

Melanie, Terrin, and Kamille we love you all and thank you for loving us and being a support for us.

Felicia Washington we thank you for your love for us and being a great accountability partner for our relationship.

Nicole Lester, what can we say? This book would not be here had it not been for you and your help with edits and having a listening ear. We needed you and you were there even when others weren't.

Ben and Michelle Hill, thank you for continuing to support us and our mission and truly helping to keep us focused to get the book completed. Your support will help so many other couples be blessed who may not have seen our message if we had not completed the book

To our couple friends who help show us in their daily walk what it means to love being married and continue to inspire us, Bernard and Dana Haynes and Kenneth and Naseera Chong.

Pia and Nimon thank you for your love and support and being the magical fantasy Aunt and Uncle for the girls and being our sister and brother.

Rev. Dr. Wesley and Rev. Dr. Rose Marie Greene thank you so much for being a shining example for us of what a loving and long-lasting marriage should look like.

Chrissi Major, thank you so much for your efforts in getting the book cover and the other artistic elements done for us. I know at times you had to be frustrated with us, but we appreciate your diligence and commitment to help put a visual to our vision.

Kenny Pugh thanks for being you, setting a great example and freely supporting us and the completion of this book. Thanks Nupie.

INTRODUCTION

We are The Marriage Coaches and we love being married. That's how we used to introduce and end the radio show we had a few years ago. We started our own movement for happy marriages in the first year of our marriage. We began in our church by highlighting couples who had been married for many years and asking them on a Sunday morning what they believed couples needed to know to make marriage work.

When we think back on this, we started this for two reasons, one being selfish and the other to truly help other couples. Our selfish reasoning was that at the time, we had what some would call a pretty adversarial relationship. Here's a little peak inside:

Alisha Says:

Two marriages, when I say that people think I mean that I've been married two times, but in actuality it means my husband and I of 15 years have had two types of marriage. In the beginning, our marriage was fraught with arguing, crying, yelling, screaming, days on end of not speaking only to repeat the cycle over again. We would argue about what, I don't know, at least once a week sometimes more. Sometimes the arguments would end with us making up and things being peaceful and then others would end with us not speaking for days on end until another argument was sparked. At the time, neither one of us really had any conflict management skills and came to the table with selfish motives of how we wanted the marriage to work. My husband was of the mindset that no matter what, we were going to stick it out and work through. Honestly on my part, I wasn't so sure. There were plenty of times that I felt like Harriet Tubman on the Underground Railroad wanting to dig my way to freedom in the middle of the night. I wanted to run away. I felt that if all we were going to do was argue and be mad at each other, what was the use in being married? Who wants to be married when all you do is argue? I know I didn't. And there was at least one time I did try to run away. (I'll tell you that story later) I couldn't run away from our problems. We had to work them out.

Ben Says:

Mind you I never went behind her, nor did I call. I knew she would be back and we would work it out. I had promised God that I would do whatever it takes to make my marriage work. You see, both my parents have been married 3 times and I vowed to myself and God that divorce is not an option. I made this covenant with God before I made a decision to walk down the aisle. I wasn't sure if my future children could handle what I had to go through, different step parents, different rules, and different expectations. I wasn't sure if they would have been strong enough. My intentions, in the beginning weren't purely spiritual. What I have found though over time is that I agree with my wife, we did have two marriages.

In the beginning I was reacting on the knowledge that I had, with no true guidance, no disrespect to my parents. I thank them for those childhood experiences because they taught me what not to do in a marriage. It wasn't until I took inventory of myself that I was better able to understand what my wife meant by two marriages. Once I got closer to God and understood my roles and responsibilities as a husband, that's when everything changed for the better. No it wasn't and isn't perfect, but it was a GREAT improvement because what I have realized on my journey is that wives want to be led by a man who is led by something greater than himself and not by his own selfish motives.

We Say:

Fast forward to year four when we moved to Georgia and we as Joel Osteen says, got into a bible-based church and began to walk out our marriage according to biblical principles. Our church at the time was moving in a direction that was growing the men up to lead and be leaders in their homes and the church. Ben began to go to the men's meetings and was being held accountable for his actions as a husband, leader, protector, and provider of our home. It forced both of us to do things a lot differently and by year 5 we were teaching pre-marital classes together by infusing our practical, biblical and Alisha's counseling experiences together to give people a no holds barred experience of what a real marriage looks like.

Overall, we learned that trials are designed to make us and our marriage stronger and we've grown from the issues in our marriage. We learned to communicate and effectively deal with our conflicts. We also learned to allow God to grow us up so that we can be better people for ourselves and each other. Yes marriage is hard and it takes a lot of hard work, but it can also be the most fulfilling relationship you've ever had.

This is our personal journey of how we have gotten to this point and we've shared this so that you can see we aren't sugar coating what marriage can really look like. This book is filled with practical, biblical and counseling tools to help you repair, restore or revitalize your relationship. It's written from both of our points of view so there will be times that Ben will be speaking directly to you and then there will be times that Alisha will be speaking directly to you.

We encourage you to read the book with your spouse and do the exercises with them. However, if your spouse does not want to do that, you can read the book just share the exercises with them. We want you to press forward and complete the book and the exercises so you can join us at the end of the book in the I Love Being Married Movement. Make a commitment today and find out how by the end of the book. Good luck on your journey, we can't wait to see you on the other side!

STAGE ONE

ASSESS YOUR MARRIAGE

CHAPTER ONE

Do You Fight for Your Marriage or Flee?

Has there ever been a time in your marriage where you were ready to give up, where you thought nothing would change and you wanted to just wave the white flag and surrender? Have you ever felt like walking away but one thing or another, kids, family, religion, values kept you from leaving? Then, after you stayed, you regretted it. There are many people who are married and have had that time where they felt like … this can't be it. I WANT OUT! If you have felt this way, you are normal and you should join the ranks of all of us who have felt the same way.

In the early years of our marriage, every time we would have one of our knock down drag out arguments, I would always feel like I was ready to go and would calculate how I would be better off by myself and I could take care of my baby by myself, and I would tell myself, plenty of other women did it every day. (Now let me clarify, a knock down drag out means it was a really bad argument with yelling, screaming, and crying. We never used physical violence to get our point across.) During our first year of marriage, I had a pretty rough time adjusting to being married and taking care of not only myself but also a husband and two children. One day after feeling like I had had enough, I packed up my bags and my baby and headed over to my parent's house. They lived, at the time, maybe 10 minutes away. Essentially, I was running away from home. Once I got there, my mom let me in, but she told me, " you can stay here tonight, but tomorrow you have to go home, we don't condone that!" Can you believe that? My parents were telling me I couldn't stay. I had to go back home to my husband and work it out. They were putting me out! Now of course they sized me up and asked if I was okay first and once they assessed that I was and we had just had a falling out they sent me on my merry way. At the time I couldn't believe this, but when looking back on it, this was probably one of the best things they could have ever done for me because I was making a permanent decision based on a temporary situation. Well anyway, the next day I went back home and we continued to have problems but we also continued to work on them. We went through some rough patches but we decided to continue working on our marriage.

During this stage of our marriage, I had a hardened heart. The bible talks about this in Mark 10:5. Jesus was talking to the Pharisees who were questioning him about divorce. Jesus responded that the time they were referring to, Moses only permitted them to divorce because of a hardened heart. However, he went on to explain that was never God's intention for marriage. He explained that his intention for marriage was for one man and one woman to be joined as one, never to be separated. The bible also explains in Malachi 2:13-16 that God hates divorce and only speaks of infidelity as a reason for divorce. The bible says in Malachi 2:16b (NLT) "To divorce your wife is to overwhelm her with cruelty". Wow can you believe that, to divorce is to overwhelm with cruelty.

We all know someone who has gone through a divorce and the pain and anguish that is dealt with prior to the split and then the venom that is spewed after the split. When you picture those couples that you know or have seen go through a divorce, doesn't it seem cruel the way that they treat one another. It is painful, hurtful; it is like a death as one person described it. If this is true, then why have you and so many of us thought about the option of divorce in our marriage? Why would we think that the decision to divorce would make it any better, when from the beginning, God told us that divorce was cruel. Why would we intentionally put ourselves through such pain and anguish? Well, we do so because we have a hardened heart and we believe that ending the relationship would be easier or would make us happier than to stay and try to work things out. Now we're not saying that anyone should put themselves in harm's way by staying in a marriage where they are being abused. Certainly, you should get to a safe place away from your abuser. Nor are we saying to those people who have divorced that their life is over. Our God is a forgiving God and will if only asked. We are the ones who don't forgive and continue to torment ourselves.

People think that divorce will make them happier, when in fact studies show the opposite. Divorce does not make you happier. People give all kinds of reasons for divorce which run the gamut from we just grew apart to I was no longer happy. Whatever reasons that are given after the fact of divorce, there had to be some issues that led up to the divorce in the first place. A scholar by the name of Dr. John Gottman talks about

19

four predictors of divorce, which are criticism, defensiveness, contempt and stonewalling. In his studies with thousands of couples he has found that these four issues predict divorce 90% of the time. Can you believe that they predicted divorce in his studies 90% of the time? Of the four, he found in his work that contempt was the #1 predictor of divorce. Just let that sit for a minute.

Many people say, if I only knew what to do beforehand, I might have been able to save my marriage. Well, this **IS** the information that you need to know beforehand! We're going to give you a few definitions to help you understand why these four can be so deadly to a relationship.

According to Webster's Dictionary, criticism is defined as criticism of a character flaw, act of making judgments, and character flaws. For example, you criticize your wife for not being as tidy as you and put yourself in a superior position whenever you bring it to her attention as if she is a child. An example of this for us would be when my husband used to say, "what you fail to understand is". Ooooh that used to burn me! If he wanted to start a fight with me all he would have to do is say that to me. Those words made me feel like a child and he was scolding me. Not a good position for your wife to be in.

Defensiveness denies responsibility to protect the character. A common way of defensiveness is whining. Both people feel they're ok and it's the other person's fault. If my husband was the criticizer, then I was the whiner. Whenever, he would speak to me like a child, I would revert to that place of being a child and begin to cry and whine and blame him, instead of taking responsibility for my part in the situation. So because I was so defensive, everything he said upset me even when he was not in the criticizer role. Can you see how this would wear on someone and create a negative dance with your spouse?

According to John Gottman, stonewalling is the absence of the listener, turning away, closing the body, no eye contact, glancing brief looks, no speaking, no facial expressions. Stonewalling can be a way of self-soothing and calming down. You know how people look when they are on their i-pod and not really focused on their surroundings except to look up occasionally, that's what stonewalling looks like in a relationship when one person is talking and the other is doing the i-pod stare. They're not really paying attention; they are zoned out to soothe themselves from the current situation or conflict.

Gottman says contempt is the escalation of criticism. This is any complaint that puts you on a higher plain than the spouse. Name calling and saying things that hurt the spouse or facial features or body gestures can display contempt. The dictionary's definition of contempt is the feeling toward someone or something one considers low, worthless; the condition of being despised; scorn, derision, disdain, hatred. Do you see the negativity connected with contempt? If you have contempt for the one you married, or you hate the one you married, can you see how that could cause many problems? Contempt is insidious. It creeps into your relationship one unresolved issue at a time. When there is a continuous unresolved issue that you feel should be resolved, you begin to resent the other person. This comes from disappointments of expectations not being met, having a negative perception of your spouse, seeing your spouse as selfish.

Now how many of us have said, I can't believe he just did that, "he is so selfish, I can't stand him"? Have you said, "she is so selfish, I don't want to deal with her nagging. She is only concerned with what she wants"? Have you ever mumbled under your breath or even said out loud, "I hate you"? It just takes one thought to play over and over enough in your mind that you begin to believe it.

Contempt is the area of a relationship where you hold grudges. She did something to you (or so you thought) so now you do something to her; tit for tat. She made you angry so now you are going to do something to show her how badly she hurt you. When you see him, you get this bad taste in your mouth; you even take on the facial expression as if you just smelled something foul in the air. When the two of you speak about an issue that has been touchy for you, you could probably cut the tension with a knife, and there is a level of hostility in the room. You may even say that your wife has been giving you the cold shoulder or she is being cold toward you.

Do you now or have you ever had any of these four issues come up in your marriage? Have you now or have you ever felt contempt for your spouse? Have you ever accused them of being selfish and only wanting their way? Do you feel like there is a barrier between the two of you that needs to be moved? Do you feel like you really don't have any of these problems and you want to make sure to keep it that way? How then do you make the necessary changes or ensure that this doesn't happen in your marriage?

One defense in this area is to resign that divorce is not an option. You can't have one foot in the door and one foot out. It will never work that way. You have to ensure that even through the rough times that you are there. Even when she appears unlovable, you decide to remain.

If contempt or hate is the #1 predictor of divorce, what should you do now if this is rearing its ugly head in your relationship? Well, we're glad you asked. The opposite emotion of contempt is devotion, friendship, affection. Are any of these a part of your relationship? Do you feel devoted to your spouse? Are they devoted to you? What does your friendship look like? Do you even have a friendship? Is there any love or affection in your relationship? When was the last loving moment that you can remember? How often are those loving moments? Do the loving moments outweigh the negative moments? Here is where the work begins. Make sure you pay close attention in the chapters to come so that you can repair, restore, revitalize and renew your relationship. We are excited for your journey!

Application Questions:

1. Do you have a hardened heart? If so what has happened in your marriage to cause this?

2. Which of the four predictors, if any, play a role in your marriage?

3. What are you willing to do at this point to make your marriage work?

Be willing to:

1. Put in the work at this stage.

2. Resign that divorce is not an option.

Ask God:

To soften your heart for your spouse so that you can see your spouse in a positive light and help you get ready to work to renew your mind.

CHAPTER TWO

What's Your Marriage Story?

How do you feel about your marriage? Be honest. The only way this will work is if you go with your first reaction to that question. How do you think your spouse feels about being married to you? If you had it to do all over again, would you marry the same person, someone else, or not at all? How do you think your spouse would answer? How would you know? Are you paying enough attention to know how they feel? Every marriage goes through rough patches; it's what you do with those rough patches that make a difference. You can say to yourself, I know we are having a hard time but I am willing to work it out or you can say this is too rough and I don't want to work it out. Sometimes you can have both. I remember times after a really huge argument in the beginning of our marriage that I wanted to give up and there was a time I did, as I told you about in the beginning of our marriage. Even then I came back after only one night. Obviously, that wasn't in God's plans for us.

Evaluating where you are in your marriage helps you know what you are dealing with so that you can work on the right issue. We are going to use a few tools in this chapter to help you assess where your relationship is right now so that you will be able to create some goals for the repair, restoration, or revitalization of your relationship.

Marriage is like a house that needs to be built on a firm foundation in order to remain stable. However, at times there are things that attack the foundation of your relationship and you need to make some repairs. Some relationships have so much damage from the termites in their lives or from the water damage that have come from the hurricanes in your life that your marriage needs restoration. Then others don't have either and have a pretty firm foundation but they still want to improve on the existing structure by adding a new room, updating the bathroom or the kitchen and revitalizing the existing structure because for the most part it works.

1. What story do you tell yourself about marriage? (for example: all marriages end in divorce, all men eventually cheat, marriage is like having a ball and chain, marriage is a blessed union ordained by God, all marriages have issues, but we can work it out)

   _____

   _____

   _____

   _____

   _____

   _____

_____

_____

2. What story do you tell yourself about **YOUR** marriage? (everything is good, even though we argue all the time, we don't have to have sex consistently to have a good marriage, my marriage has survived some storms and we are stronger for it)

_____

_____

_____

_____

_____

_____

_____

_____

3. What has been the most troubling time in your marriage? On a scale of 1 – 10, how would you rank your marriage overall at that time. (With 1 being the lowest and 10 being the highest)

_____

_____

_____

_____

_____

_____

_____

4. How does your marriage now compare to the most troubling time you've had in your marriage?

_____

_____

_____

_____

_____

_____
_____
_____

5. What has been the happiest time in your marriage? On a scale of 1 – 10, how would you rank your marriage overall at that time. (With 1 being the lowest and 10 being the highest)

_____
_____
_____
_____
_____
_____
_____

6. How does your marriage now compare to the happiest time in your marriage?

_____
_____
_____
_____
_____
_____
_____
_____
_____
_____

7. On a scale of 1-10, how would you rank your marriage overall **NOW**? (With 1 being the lowest and 10 being the highest)

_____

_____

_____

8. How do you feel about how your marriage now
    compared to the most troubling time?

_____

_____

_____

_____

_____

_____

_____

_____

9. How do you feel about how your marriage now
    compared to the happiest time?

_____

_____

_____

_____

_____

_____

_____

_____

_____

The previous questions will help you get a realistic view of how you feel about your marriage so that you can have a better assessment of where you are currently in your marriage and where you want to go. The following assessments will dig a little deeper into what issues or concerns you may have and want to improve.

In business, leaders have used the SWOT Analysis to make an analysis of the current structure of their business and the same analysis could be used to analyze your relationship. SWOT stands for strengths, weaknesses, opportunities, and threats.

The strengths in your relationship are those things that add to the relationship and are what keeps the relationship strong. For example, a strength could be your ability to communicate about many different topics, your friendship with one another, or that you have a great sexual relationship.

Weaknesses are those things that need to be addressed so that they don't get out of hand and attack your foundation. For example, you and your wife are able to communicate well, but whenever you are upset with her and try to communicate that to her she begins to cry before you can even get it out. Weaknesses are those things that can turn into threats if you do not address them.

Opportunities are those things that you do to enhance or improve your relationship, but have not yet taken the time to do so. For example, your husband has been saying how much he wants to spend a night alone with you for the last month, but neither one of you have taken the time to find a babysitter for the kids to make this happen. Opportunities not taken can also turn into threats because resentments build up and corrode away at the opportunities that present themselves.

Threats are those things that can literally rock the core of your foundation. For example, that woman at work who has been eyeballing you even though she knows that you are married. That debt that you have that is choking the life out of any dream that you may have had or the newly diagnosed illness of your child. Again, a threat is anything that can shock the foundation of your relationship. Use the chart below to do a SWOT analysis of your relationship by writing about any current strengths, weaknesses, opportunities or threats.

Strengths	Weaknesses
What are your strengths that you and others describe as an asset? What do you do well? What can you do to help manage your home and move your family forward?	Is there something that you have handled in the past that hasn't worked well? Is there something that you and others have said you need to improve? What are some things that you've done repeatedly that has sparked disagreements or caused you to feel defensive in your marriage?
Opportunities	Threats
What opportunities are present in your marriage that you could be capitalizing on if you let go of those areas you either don't like to do or are your weakness? Where can you provide the skills needed to move your family forward?	What are those things that cause a threat to the foundation of your family? What are those things that if not dealt with could harm your relationship? Could any of your weaknesses cause serious harm to your family if not improved?

Now we would like you to assess your relationship based on the 10 areas we believe comprise a successful relationship. *In the graph on page 37, shade in the column for each separate category based on a scale from 1 – 10, with one being the lowest and ten being the highest. One would be at the bottom and 10 would be at the top and 5 would be mid way. We will do this for each area. The questions asked under each of the 9 categories will help to assess your thoughts and feelings for each thus you are giving an overall ranking for each category*. For example even though there are 3 questions under acceptance, you will only give one final rank under that column in the graph provided. We have placed extra copies of the graph in the appendix so that you can assess your relationship and have your spouse do so as well. After reading the book and implementing the steps you and your spouse can then reassess how you feel using the extra copies of the graphs.

Acceptance

On a scale of 1 – 10, how much do you accept your spouse for who they are, just as they are today? Do you accept their flaws and their differences from you? Do you accept that they were raised differently from you and come from a different background? This question speaks to the ego in all of us that makes us think that the best way for our spouse to be is to be just like us. How absurd! If your wife was just like you there would be no need for one of you in the relationship.

Appreciation

On a scale of 1-10, how much do you appreciate your spouse? Do you take for granted what they do for you? If it were a stranger doing the same thing for you, would you say thank you?

Friendship

On a scale of 1-10, do you consider your spouse as your friend? Do you enjoy spending time with them? Do you have fun together? When you have something good happen to you is your spouse one of the first people you want to tell? Do you see your spouse as that person you can talk to when you are having a bad day or if you have had something negative happen to you? Do you see your spouse as someone who encourages you?

Love

On a scale of 1-10, do you truly love your spouse unconditionally? Would you give anything for your spouse? Do you love them above all others including your children? Does this person rank at the top of your list when you think of the people you love? Do you want to make sure that they feel loved? Are you willing to sacrifice some of your own needs and wants for them? Do you feel selfless when you do something for them?

Now this is the point that some people might get irritated and say to themselves, what about me? How do I feel? I think I'm doing a pretty good job, but my husband isn't doing his best or I am doing all I can and my wife is just so selfish. Even though you may have every legitimate reason to feel this way, in order to make positive changes in your relationship, you have to focus on what you can change, which is yourself. You can't brow beat someone into changing or even seducing someone into changing, because you've already found out that it doesn't work. The only person that you truly have control over is yourself. So if you make the changes and your spouse sees that you are genuine in your changes and not coming from a selfish place, in time, they will be willing to change as well, if they are still in the fight for your marriage.

Expectations Based on What You Value

Now this one is a little awkward to explain, but this area is HUGE when it comes to marriage. This area can cause the biggest area of resentment and anger towards the other person and you may not even know where it comes from. On a scale of 1-10, do you feel like your spouse meets your expectations for what you think a husband or a wife should be according to what you value? For example, many people value the husband as being the head of the household and that is something that you want for your marriage, but your husband won't take the lead and you feel like all of the family's burdens fall on your shoulders. Another example is that many people value that the mother is the primary caregiver for the children, but your wife doesn't seem to have that maternal instinct and seems to shirk what you see as motherly duties. A lot of people avoid conversations about expectations because they feel that it could lead to an argument. Expectations are things that we have either grown up seeing in our homes or not seeing in our homes that we have found value in and want our spouses to fulfill these expectations. However, if these expectations are never spoken then how does your spouse know that this is something that you value?

Forgiveness

On a scale of 1-10, do you feel like you have forgiven your spouse for any issues that have come up in your marriage? Is there anything that you may be holding a grudge on?

Trust

On a scale of 1 – 10, do you trust your spouse? Do you trust your spouse with your finances implicitly? Do you trust your spouse with your heart? This is a deep question, especially if there has been infidelity in this relationship or if you have been hurt in this relationship or even in a past relationship. People don't realize how much baggage they bring from past relationships into present relationships. Is your spouse paying for the sins of someone else? Do you trust your spouse is being truthful with you? Do you trust their intentions and motivation? Do you think that they are unselfish in the decisions that they make? If you have doubt in any of these areas, you have some level of a trust issues with your spouse?

Communication

On a scale of 1 – 10, are the two of you able to communicate and come to some resolution at the end of the conversation? How well do you deal with conflict? Are you and your spouse able to decrease conflict? Are you able to bring up touchy issues and talk about it without things getting out of hand? Are you and your spouse able to problem-solve?

Sex

On a scale of 1-10, how satisfied are you with your sex life? Sex is a form of communication that allows the two to become one physically. It is a time to commune with one another. When was the last time that you and your spouse communicated sexually? Do you feel like the way you communicate sexually expresses how you really feel about your spouse?

Spirituality

On a scale of 1- 10, is spirituality a part of your marital relationship? If it is, to what degree? Do you allow God to be a part of your relationship? Do you see your spouse as a gift that God has given to you? Do you see yourself as a steward or caretaker of this person this gift that God has given to you? Does your relationship with God influence how you treat your spouse?

As you can see these areas are complex and will require some work on your part to bring them up to the point that you deem to be a ten. However, you can also have your spouse go through the book as well to assess how they feel about your marriage. You can also read the book with your spouse so that the two of you can work on it together. Those of you that are not married can use the book as a tool to help you prepare for the time when you do decide to marry.

All of these questions have been geared toward how you feel about your marriage? What we want to know is, and surely you do too, how does your spouse feel about your relationship? What would they have to say about you if they were asked these questions? How do they view you? What would they say about you behind your back if they knew you would never find out? Would what they had to say be negative or positive? If you are not sure, now would be a good time to ask.

Walker Marriage Assessment Tool (2.2)

Acceptance	Appreciation	Friendship	L o v e	Forgiveness	Expectations	T r u s t	Communication	S e x	Spirituality

Now that you have shaded in the table, you can see there are some areas that you see as pretty positive, they may be as much as a 7 or higher. If an area is a 6 or below, there needs to be some work done on that specific area.

In this example, this couple has several areas that need to be dealt with. This person has ranked the acceptance scale at a 2, appreciation scale at a 2, the friendship scale at a 5, the love scale at a 3, the expectations at a 7, the trust at a 9, the forgiveness scale at a 3, the communication at a 1, the sex at a 6, and the spirituality at a1. As you can see most areas of the marriage need to be worked on. However, there is no need for alarm or a reason to feel overwhelmed as you can see there are some highlights in this marriage. There are some positives that need to be celebrated. That is exactly where this person needs to start, an appreciation and a celebration of the successes and positives in their marriage. However, after the celebration comes the work.

In making changes we need to celebrate any milestones that are met. Each area that is a 6 or below needs to addressed. However, you will only deal with one issue at a time. To deal with one issue at a time you will need to rank each issue in order of priority of or the area that needs the most care. This is done so that you can prioritize the areas that you would like to work on so that you don't feel overwhelmed. Even for those couples who have a pretty solid foundation, there is always something that could use an improvement and this is a great way to tease the areas out that you would like to work on.

Acceptance	Appreciation	Friendship	Love	Forgiveness	Expectations	Trust	Communication	Sex	Spirituality

1. Rank your top 3 concerns, with the #1 issue being the one that if corrected and can correct others.

   _____

   _____

   _____

2. After you have ranked them, take the one that you have ranked as the #1 issue, the one you saw as urgent, the issue that if you worked on it could possibly affect one or two others. Write down which one that is here.

   _____

   _____

3. Could any of the areas that are 6 or below fall under a weakness or a threat from your SWOT Analysis? If so, how?

   _____

   _____

   _____

   _____

   _____

   _____

   _____

4. How can these issues you've ranked as your top issues as a weakness or a threat negatively impacting your marriage?

   _____

_____

_____

_____

_____

_____

_____

_____

_____

5. What can you do to improve the issue you ranked as the #1 issue within the next seven days by just a half point?

_____

_____

_____

_____

_____

_____

_____

For example, in this scenario, this person has two issues that are at a level one; communication and spirituality. This person has chosen the communication as her #1 issue and she feels is the most urgent, because it permeates every area of her life with her spouse. After communication was chosen, this person needs to ask herself, what can I do within the next 7 days to make the communication better between me and my spouse, by just half a point? How can I go from a 1 to a 1½? Well, think of the top thing in this area that your spouse complains about when the two of you communicate. In this scenario, the husband complains that his wife talks too long and too much when they are talking. In this instance, if she would cut down on the length of time that she talks about any one issue and limit the time to just one hour for overall discussion, she can time herself to not talk more than 5 minutes at a time during the discussion. By doing just one of these examples, she could improve the rank of her score at least a half point in one week. We call this speaking in bite-sized pieces so that you don't choke the listener with the information that you are sharing. Too much of anything is overwhelming. Of course any new skill takes time and practice, but it can be done. Find something that is tangible, something that you can realistically do within the next 7 days and that you are confident that you can achieve.

Now that you have figured out which issue is the most important and you have figured out what you can do within the next 7 days to improve in that area by just a half point, you are ready to put your plan into action. Concentrate on this one area specifically and pay close attention to whether or not you are falling back into the old behavior that you are trying to change. Keep a log of the number of times in the next 7 days you have changed the specific behavior you identified that will help you move your score by at least a half point. Become aware of the behavior and then work to change it no matter how your spouse acts or reacts. Remember, you can't change someone else, you can only change yourself. Ultimately, when your spouse sees you putting forth some effort, they will too, if they still see the marriage as a worthwhile investment.

As you're moving through the book, we will come back to the issues that you have expressed here and compare your scores from this chapter so that you can see in black and white whether there really is any improvement. Being able to do this can help you truly see the progress that is being made. This will also help you see how you have improved in the areas you saw as a challenge as well as the overall improvement in how you ranked your marriage today.

Application Questions:

1. Are you being realistic about the state your relationship is in?

2. What will you do within the next 7 days to bring about a positive change for your relationship?

3. How will your marriage change, now that you understand the strengths, weaknesses, opportunities and threats to your relationship?

4. Are you willing to move forward at this time and put in the work even if your spouse isn't?

Be willing to:

1. Assess your part in the relationship and the state that it is in.

2. Be honest about how you feel about your spouse and your relationship.

3. Put in the work to work on you even if your spouse is not ready. You only have the power to change you.

Ask God:

To reveal what your role is in the relationship. To convict you when you try to blame your spouse for your flaws or issues that you may have created. To prepare you for the work that is to come.

STAGE TWO

SETTING THE STAGE FOR CHANGE

CHAPTER THREE

Time to Change the Game

Have you ever thought about what it would be like if you could change your marriage? What it would take? How much work it would require? Would you have the energy to do so? Do you even think that your marriage is worth it? If you are willing to work on it, is your spouse willing to work on it? If you do the work will your spouse even notice? Will your spouse participate in making the marriage better? What if you do all this work and they remain the same? Would you still be willing?

In this chapter we will deal with the ABCs of change. In this model, A stands for attitude, B stands for belief (thoughts and feelings), and C stands for choice. In the previous chapters we talked about the negative side of marriage and all the things that can lead to divorce if not dealt with. Then, we asked you to assess how you felt about your relationship and the specific areas that can lead to a loving marriage. Now, in this chapter, we will deal with how to change your mind from the negative to the positive and what are the necessary steps to do so.

There are many schools of thought about how to make changes come about. One of them is biblical. The bible says in Proverbs 23:7, For as a man thinks in his heart, so is he. (New King James Version)In recent years, there has been much talk about The Law of Attraction and how your thoughts whether positive or negative draw positive or negative energy to you and render you positive or negative results. Basically, both are saying that if you think negatively then negative things will be what you focus on, thus negative results will be what you receive. However, on the other hand, if you think positively, then positive things will be what you focus on, thus positive results will be what you receive. The way you perceive issues in your life determines how you will react in any given situation. If you always view a situation or a person as negative then that situation or person will become that for you.

In any given situation, there is always an act (A) that precedes your beliefs (B), thoughts and feelings surrounding that act and finally once the beliefs are formed whether consciously or unconsciously, a choice (C) is made. In the belief section is where the change begins in how you view your spouse and your marriage. At this point some people will say, it can't be that easy I don't believe that just the act of changing my beliefs will ultimately change my choices and how I feel about my spouse. Let's break this down with a few scenarios. In each scenario, the act preceding what you believe, think, and feel stays the same in both the positive and the negative scenarios. The change comes in the Belief stage. Once you change your beliefs, thoughts and feelings about the other person, you are able to make a positive choice that will stay in line with how you feel. You are giving your spouse the benefit of the doubt that their intention around the act that they did was not a negative one. Even if their intention was negative, the fact that you realize that you can only make changes for yourself and are taking responsibility for your actions can be a game changer. Here are a couple of examples:

1. **NEGATIVE**

   A. Act – I leave a messy desk after 2 weeks of doing ok after a discussion of how Ben cannot deal with clutter and I agree to make some changes.
   B. Belief- Ben takes a negative view; He thinks I have done this on purpose because I know this bothers him.
   C. Choice – Ben makes the choice to throw away my papers based on his negative perception of my act. He then proceeds to tell me that I fail to understand how leaving a messy desk irritates him and tells me what a poor housekeeper I am and how lazy and selfish I am. (His comments are full of criticism and contempt, which as you may recall from chapter 1 are 2 fatal signs of a marriage in trouble)

   POSITIVE

   A. Act – I leave a messy desk after 2 weeks of doing ok after a discussion
   B. Belief – Ben takes a positive view; He realizes that I have been trying and that change does not come over night.
   C. Choice – Ben makes the choice to in a positive light; He asks if I need any help to organize my papers because he noticed after 2 weeks of doing well, I was starting to slip backwards. (This time his comments had no judgment, no criticism, and no contempt)

2. **NEGATIVE**

   A. Act - You have asked your spouse for sex the last three nights and your spouse has turned you down each time.
   B. Belief – She just doesn't want to have sex with me because she is selfish. (contempt)She is always holding out me. If she only knew that this new woman at work is checkin me out, I bet she would give me some then. (thought) I am so angry, irritated, frustrated, and fed up. (feeling)
   C. Since she won't give me any sex, I won't help her with the kids. Maybe after she sees how it feels to want something and don't get it, she will give me some.

   POSITIVE

   A. Act - You have asked your spouse for sex the last three nights and your spouse has turned you down each time.
   B. Belief – I know that she is tired because she has put in extra hours at work and our youngest has been sick. I understand.
   C. Choice – You ask your spouse is there anything you can do to help relieve some of the pressure that she has been under because it has been a while since the two of you have communicated sexually and you would love to make love to her.

3. **NEGATIVE**

   A. Act - You want to go out on a date night regularly, but your spouse just can't seem to find the time.
   B. Belief - He is just being selfish. He knows how much I like to get out, just the two of us. He is just doing this to be spiteful, to get back at me. (thought) I can't stand him. (feeling) (contempt)
   C. Choice – I know he is doing this on purpose. I'm just gonna make sure that when it's time for him to go out

with his boys, I will conveniently forget and make sure I am nowhere to be found so that he has to watch the kids.

POSITIVE

A. Act - You want to go out on a date night regularly, but your spouse just can't seem to find the time.
B. Belief – Time has been short lately with all of the changes in our life. Maybe we can wait until things calm down to go out on a date.
C. Choice - You talk to your spouse and explain how much quality time means to you. The two of you decide to schedule a time in the near future that you can spend time alone without distractions even if that means you have to spend time at home.

4. **NEGATIVE**

A. Act – Your spouse continues to spend money that you don't have even after a discussion about your budget.
B. Belief – She is being selfish. She is only thinking of herself. If she continues to spend like this, she will put us in the poor house. She is so clueless when it comes to money. I will have to teach her a lesson.
C. Choice – Since she can't control her spending, I will control it for her. I will open a new account that she does not have access to and leave only enough for household items in the joint account. I bet she'll learn her lesson after that.

POSITIVE

A. Act – Your spouse continues to spend money that you don't have even after a discussion about your budget.

B. Belief – I have a better understanding about money and she may need help in seeing how her actions affect our household.

C. Choice – You create a budget to show your spouse what you can really afford and the two of you agree on a weekly spending plan to help her stay within budget.

If you view situations and people in a positive or healthy light, then situations and people will be seen as positive, thus you will gain positive results. Look at some of these scenarios that were set out for you. In example one, what would have happened if Ben had really thrown out my papers, when I was working on something because he thought that I was leaving a messy desk to be selfish? What if it was the notes for this book? In Scenario 2, what would have happened if the man would have not helped out with the kids and acted on his belief that the woman at work was checkin him out? What damage could have been done, because he believed that she was holding out on him to be spiteful?

In Scenario 3, what would have happened if she would have intentionally made sure she wasn't available when it was time for the husband to leave?

In Scenario 4 what would have happened if the husband had transferred all of the funds except what was necessary for the household because he wanted to teach her a lesson?

Do you see how all of these are tit for tat situations and can create a nasty dance that will only continue to escalate? The escalation of these can lead to contempt, the #1 predictor of divorce if left unchecked. However, just by being aware of your beliefs, thoughts, and feelings, you can consciously make the choice to think positively about your spouse, give them the benefit of the doubt and decide to make a choice that is also positive. In each scenario, an even bigger argument or escalation was avoided. How would you feel if you could avoid a fight with your spouse? Wouldn't that be a load off your shoulders? I know when you're in that negative dance of she is so selfish, he is so selfish, it's hard to get out. It's like a you have signed up for the negative tango. However, you can't do that tango without a partner and if one of you decides to make the changes and put in the work, that negative venom filled tango can turn into the most beautiful dance you have ever seen.

As I have said many times, we have had two marriages, one in which we fueled our relationship based on the negative and one that was fueled on the <u>love that we have for one another and for God. Our focus on those two things instead of what the other was or was not doing turned our marriage around.</u> I'm telling you if we had stayed on that negative roller coaster much longer, the story would have been much different, because we would have been divorced after our second year of marriage. Put in the work.

I don't know who lied to us and why we bought into the lie that if we have to work at marriage or a relationship that It isn't worth it because love or marriage shouldn't be that hard. **MARRIAGE IS HARD WORK**. Marriage requires a lot from each partner, but at times one partner is putting in more work than the other. We hear you when you say well how long do I have to put in all of the work? When is my spouse gonna put in the effort? We bet if you asked them, they would say the same thing. You have got to get out of the tit for tat mentality and take responsibility for your own actions. Your actions are yours based on your beliefs, thoughts, and feelings. No one has made you make the choices that you have made. Give up the blame game of I did this because you did that. What ends up happening is someone else is always at fault and nothing is ever your fault. Does this sound familiar? This is a part of defensiveness, one of the four predictors of divorce. Take a good hard look at yourself and evaluate what you bring to the table or <u>what you don't</u>.

As Ben and I talked and began to prepare for this book the phrase, "be willing" kept coming up over and over in our conversation. It became clear to us that whatever you are being asked to do in your relationship and for your spouse, you must "be willing" to do it. If you are not a willing participant it will only look like that scene when a child is made to do something they don't want to do. You know how you were as a child when you were told to do something you either didn't want to do or were not willing to do. You poked your lips out, sucked your teeth, and did the opposite to make your parents mad so that they would just give in. Maybe you were in a more active rebellion later on where you even ran away either mentally, physically, or emotionally when it was something you didn't want to do or were not willing to deal with. Does it feel like that now with what we are asking you to do? If so then you are not a willing participant. We can want all day for you to have a great marriage or a great relationship, however, if you are not willing to do the work then we certainly can't make it magically appear.

Can you imagine what it would have been like if God told Jesus that He had to get on the cross for all of our sins and Jesus showed out , sulked, pouted, stomped His feet, procrastinated, prolonged? All we are saying here is that you must be willing to put these practices into place so that you can have a fruitful relationship and or develop the skills needed when you do find that person you want to be in relationship with.

Renew Your Mind

Not only do you need to give each other the benefit of the doubt, you must be willing. Be willing to: trust, forgive, apologize, love, see the good, fight for your marriage, accept when you're wrong, make changes when necessary, compromise, listen to the other's opinion, do the good thing even when you don't feel like it, sacrifice for your spouse, to turn the negative in your relationship into something positive, and use those bad times as a way for you to appreciate the good times. What we're asking you to do here is renew your mind. The bible speaks of the renewal of the mind in Romans 12:2. **The Amplified Bible says in** Romans 12:1-2

2Do not be conformed to this world (this age), [fashioned after and adapted to its external, superficial customs], but be transformed (changed) by the [entire] renewal of your mind [by its new ideals and its new attitude], so that you may prove [for yourselves] what is the good and acceptable and perfect will of God, even the thing which is good and acceptable and perfect [in His sight for you].

This verse is saying for you to change by the renewing of your mind in its ideals and attitudes. In order to do this you have to be able to change how think about things. You have to renew you mind to counteract the negative with the positive and transform into the image of Christ by using the Holy Spirit as a filter of how you will react.

In our counseling sessions, groups and classes, we always say the way you speak to or treat your spouse should be in a way that is respectful. Would talk to or treat Jesus the way you do your spouse? If the answer is no, then you shouldn't treat your spouse that way. For those people who can't relate to that scenario, would you talk to or treat your boss the way you do your spouse? Again, if the answer is no, then you shouldn't treat your spouse that way. Make your marriage a priority. Anything worth having takes work. Remember what you loved about one another before all of life's complications.

Hurdles (transitions) are chances to enhance your relationship. How will you appreciate the good with no bad? Bad times can bring you closer if you learn to work as a team. Change your thinking to, two are better than one. It's the I got your back mentality. [12] A person standing alone can be attacked and defeated, but two can stand back-to-back and conquer. Three are even better, for a triple-braided cord is not easily broken. (Ephesians 7:12 NLT)

Creating a new mind set does take time; you are forming a new habit. At this time, we want you to create note cards or sticky notes for yourself so that you can be reminded to 1) Renew my mind daily 2) Choose the positive 3)I Love Being Married. This last statement may be a lot for you at this time. However, again, this is forming a new mind set. We are asking you to focus on this renewed mind set so that after a period of time of reading and speaking out loud the statement I Love Being Married, you will be able to make this statement a part of your reality.

Application Questions:

1. What will you do today to renew your mind about your spouse?
2. Where can you give your spouse the benefit of the doubt?

3. Is there a recent situation that you could use the ABC method to change your outlook on something your spouse has done?
4. What steps are you willing to take to help you move one step closer to being able to say, I love being married?

Be willing to:

1. Renew your mind.

2. Choose the positive

3. Speak out loud daily, I Love Being Married, even if at this time, you don't.

Ask God:

To renew your mind so that you can begin to see your spouse in a positive light and help you explore the things that made you fall in love with your spouse in the first place.

CHAPTER FOUR

Accepting Your Spouse, Flaws and All

Ok now that we've talked about how you change, what do you do when you and your spouse do try to change? What if after a period of time they are making positive strides, but something happens and they revert back to their old ways? Will that make you revert too? Will you go back to the tit for tat after they slip up? Or will you admit it when you slip up to help avoid the return to the tit for tat negativity that you once had? Leave room for mistakes. Nobody is perfect. Don't try to make your spouse a carbon copy of you. Flaws are a part of people in relationships. What would the relationship be like, honestly if it was a relationship with two of you?

What are your flaws? Would you like it if someone constantly pointed them out to you? How would you feel if they did? How would you handle that situation? Would you be able to continue to listen to that person and still respect and even love them? Are you the critical person in your relationship? How do you think your spouse feels? Is your spouse now married to their mother or their father instead of a husband or a wife?

Would you love you and then marry you with all of your flaws? How would it feel if at least one person in this world accepted you and all of the baggage that you bring to the table like that ex-wife, the kids from a previous relationship, lack of financial skills, the extra weight you put on, your stretch marks, your shyness, your talkativeness and on and on? Having someone accept you for all that you are and all that comes along with who you are takes a special person. Someone specifically fashioned for you. Someone who is willing to love you no matter what; cancer, inability to have children, job loss, death of a parent, financial hardship, illness of a child, and on and on. How would you feel if someone accepted you completely? What if you were forgiven for all of your flaws?

Everyone comes to a relationship with a past. Everyone has some sort of baggage that they bring to the table. We all have things we've said and done that we wish that we could take back, let alone asking someone else to accept these flaws that we have. However, we are asking someone else to accept us, flaws and all when we are becoming someone's wife or husband. We are asking them to accept that we come from a dysfunctional family, we come from a family with a history of mental illness, we have a family history of diabetes, or high blood pressure. We are asking this person to accept that we may not have the best financial skills, that we have a shaky relationship right now with God. We are asking them to accept our fluctuating weight, the possibility of sickness, job loss, grief and pain. We are asking our spouses to accept our past, current, and future choices. We are asking our spouses to accept us for who we are unconditionally and not try and make us a mirror image of them, when we say I do. Are you accepting your spouse unconditionally for who they are flaws and all, with all of their baggage and issues? Are they accepting of you?

Acceptance means many things, but when we speak of acceptance here, we are speaking of having an understanding way, realizing that we all got to this point with a history that trails behind us that affects all choices, feelings, and behaviors. None of us arrived at the altar from a vacuum, so why is it that once we get married so many of us expect that the person we married should be perfect all the time and if they make a mistake, it's the worst thing possible and they should be drawn and quartered? Often times when we're pointing out flaws, we're asking our spouse to change. We're asking them to conform to some ideal that we've formed in our heads that we believe is best, but best for whom? Are you really pointing out the flaw for the betterment of your spouse or is it for your benefit? If they changed that thing you've been asking for, would it make them better or is it strictly for your benefit or to make you more comfortable? The backlash to pointing out flaws comes when it appears or feels like to your spouse that all of your requests, demands, commands come from a selfish place and are only being made for your benefit. It's okay to have your desires met, but a relationship between two people can't solely be based on what you as an individual wants

Acceptance and understanding of who your spouse is and not for who you want them to be is key. So often people enter into a relationship asking their spouse to change and become a mirror image of them. If this is the case, why didn't you just stay single if you loved the way you were so much? Asking someone to change is arrogant and presupposes that your way and what you know is better than the other person and for that matter that you are better than them. So if you and your ways are better what does that make your spouse? Less than. Who wants to be considered less than? Who wants to feel like the way they handle situations are not as good as the other person? Who wants to feel like they are not as good as the other person? Who wants to be in essence chastised for the choices that they have made or for the way they act? This puts one person in a superior position and one in an inferior position. Who wants to feel inferior in their marriage? I'm sure most of you reading this have never thought about this part of your relationship in this way, but it is important to realize that our words and actions have power and truly accepting your spouse for who they are even with all of their baggage is really POWERFUL! If you don't believe us, ask your spouse how they would feel if you accepted them even with their weight, messiness, lack of financial prowess, lack of understanding of what it takes to be a husband, history of mental illness, whatever that one issue is that stands out to you and your spouse as the one thing they feel self-conscious about? The choice to accept your spouse and the actions that follow to show them that you do is a sense of relief for your spouse, a way for them to let go, release and breathe. It is truly a weight that is lifted off of their shoulders. It's the way that some of us were able to feel from our parents like we could do no wrong and even if we did, we were corrected in love and once the correction was over, they still loved us. In marriage, we just want to feel the same way that no matter what I say or do, no matter how I look; even if I got cancer tomorrow, lost all my hair and no longer looked like the woman you married, you would still love me, accept me and take care of me.

Some people, however, come from an inherently critical place because that's how they grew up. Their mom or dad was very critical of them, so that's all that they know how to do. So they are not just critical of you, they are critical of themselves. Being critical is a learned behavior, just like anything else and can be unlearned. The lack of acceptance and understanding or being overly criticized could lead to one person in the marriage feeling judged. When people feel judged, they don't feel like they can completely be themselves, they feel like they are walking on eggshells to avoid a mistake or they either begin to hide things from their spouse or begin to share them with someone else. Sometimes in an effort to make things better, we create our own monsters. For example, this was an issue with one of the couples we worked with where the husband would criticize how the wife did things. In her mind, after so much of this, she felt like the husband was judging her, which made her feel less than and not good enough. After a while, she just gave up because she felt like no matter what she did, she was going to be wrong all the time. As a result of this behavior, many people in this situation will either retreat from their spouse in order to avoid feeling judged and or begin to confide in someone else, whether that's their mother, father, sister, brother, friend or that woman or man that has been looking for the opportunity to become "friends" with your spouse. The door has been opened for someone to accept them for who they are, have great conversation and enjoy their company.

Acceptance and understanding is that missing ingredient in most marital relationships when it comes to recurring issues that come up over and over again. For example, if you and your spouse have discussed over and over again the differences in what you think tidiness in your home should look like and whenever you discuss it, you continue to get angry, you have not accepted the differences between you and your spouse. Your husband did not grow up in your home, so he doesn't have the same thought process of when you left a dish in the sink at night, your mom would wake you up to come clean it even if it was 3:00 in the morning. You learned that in order to avoid being woken up out of a deep sleep, you would just clean the dish before bed thus avoiding a consequence. On the other hand, your wife didn't grow up in your home, where your mom would make a home cooked meal every night, so she doesn't see the value of a home cooked meal every night and sees it more as a burden. We've seen both of these scenarios in many a relationship cause a problem. However, they don't have to be, if you could accept that you and your spouse are different, come from different backgrounds and bring different experiences to the table. By doing this, you can learn to celebrate the differences to create a new way of doing things in your home, together, versus what you did in your home growing up or in a previous relationship.

In order to accept someone wholeheartedly, it takes patience, gentleness, humility and tolerance. Patience is needed when dealing with acceptance because sometimes the way that your spouse handles a situation could cause a problem and you are able to see it because you are at a different vantage point. However, this is not the time to say I know how to do this so just let me do it, or if you do it that way, you are just going to fall on your face or if you sit back and let them do it their way, that is not the time to say, I told you so. Patience in the process of acceptance means I am willing to deal with the consequences and if there is something that needs to be said, I am going to say it in love. I am going to talk to my spouse in truth and in love. I am going to say what is necessary to help make the situation better and continue to love them regardless of the outcome. Handling the situation this way is being gentle as opposed to being argumentative and ridiculing them for not handling things the way you thought that they should've been handled. By adding humility to the mix you are outwardly showing through your posture that you aren't talking to or treating your spouse like they are less than. You are treating them as if they are just as important as you and what they think and feel matters to you.

When accepting someone completely, you are loving them as you would love yourself. You wouldn't intentionally say or do something to hurt yourself. You wouldn't intentionally say something to belittle how you feel or make yourself feel less than. A good filter to see whether or not you are completely accepting your spouse is to ask yourself, if that were me in this moment would I feel accepted or less than?

On the flip side, yes we are saying that to be able to move into the level of love that we will discuss in chapter 7, you must completely accept your spouse for all of who they are. We are not, however saying that you should just lay back and let your spouse's ways become the order of the day if you truly do believe they are to the detriment of your spouse, your relationship or your children. If you feel that what they are saying or doing could negatively impact your home, then by all means address it and talk to your spouse about changes that need to be made. However, this needs to be done with love and understanding, in a gentle way and in a way that doesn't feel like your spouse is being chastised. Make sure that your spouse understands that you are discussing the issue in a way that is for their betterment and the overall betterment of your family. Make them realize that you do accept them for who they are, but the behavior they're engaging in or the words that they are speaking is affecting your relationship or the family as a whole. If your spouse is coming from a place of unselfishness, they will be able to accept what you have said and will be willing to make changes. Understand that changing takes time and there will be some ebb and flow and back and forth that is done, but the change process will be helped by the two of you establishing what that change looks like and how it will affect everyone.

Acceptance means learning to understand your spouse and what makes them tick. You learn who they are inside and out. You become the expert on them so that the issue that used to really bother you doesn't bother you as much anymore because you were able to see it in context. For example, your wife likes to spend time with you and gets irritated when you don't because she grew up in a home where her dad was rarely around and when he was he didn't spend that much time with her even though that is something she desired. She felt rejected by this so now when you don't want to spend time with her, she feels rejected. Yes that's why she acts that way. How would your relationship be different now that you can put her behavior in context and acknowledge to her that you accept that her feelings of rejection stem from her relationship with her dad and that you understand how your not spending time with her reminds her of that. Your wife would then feel completely understood and you could now accept this once irritating behavior and to be quite honest her behavior helped to fuel you not wanting to spend time with her because the more she complained, the more you didn't want to spend time with her.

Become the expert on your spouse. Begin to understand why they do what they do, not just on the surface. If you do, you will begin to understand all of those behaviors that you thought just came out of the blue. You will be able to put the behaviors in context, sort of like watching a movie, its hard to understand what's going on when you come in the middle of the movie, but if you pay close enough attention, you get the context and can follow along. The good part about being in a relationship, even though you have come in the middle of the movie, you have the ability to ask questions so that you can understand them better. All of what we are asking you to do takes time, but you have to ask yourself, is my spouse worth it, is my marriage worth it? If the answer is yes, remember the energy you had when you were pursuing your mate, then use that energy now to get to know your spouse better.

Acceptance means taking into account the whole picture of your spouse's behavior because most of the time the behavior is based on a value system that you may not be aware of and one that your spouse may not be aware of either. We will discuss how these values play out in expectations in chapter 8. Acceptance means taking into account the persons flaws and loving them anyway. Flaws are cracks to the foundation and blemishes in your spouse's makeup. Acceptance and understanding of these flaws, cracks and blemishes to your spouse's foundation, to their core will make them feel completely accepted, fully loved and free to make mistakes because they know that you will love them anyway.

Application Questions:

1. Are you willing to accept your spouse's flaws?

2. Are you willing to show your spouse that you can accept and understand them completely?

3. How do you need to change your mindset so that you can accept your spouse completely?

4. Are there any barriers to accepting and understanding your spouse?

Be willing to:

1. Accept your spouse's flaws

2. See them as imperfect people

3. Hold them to the standard that you are only willing to be held to yourself

4. See their flaws as unique to them and if they weren't there, you would be married to someone else

5. Help them to make changes when necessary from an unselfish place for their benefit

Ask God:

To convict you when you are pointing out a flaw of your spouse with the wrong motive (not for the betterment of your spouse, unselfish, but for your benefit, selfish). To help you accept and understand your partner's flaws and help you love your spouse despite their flaws and that they can love you despite your flaws.

CHAPTER FIVE

Do You Really See the Best in Your Spouse?

When was the last time you said thank you to your spouse? When was the last time you pampered your wife to show her that you love and appreciate her, just for her benefit and not for your benefit? When was the last time you showed your appreciation for your husband without having another motive behind it? How often do you give words of appreciation or even little gifts? Has your spouse done something special lately and you didn't even acknowledge it? Have you acknowledged and appreciated the little things that your spouse has done even the ones that you think they "should" be doing anyway? I know you've heard, you don't get credit for the things you're supposed to do anyway, but what if you did? Would it encourage you to want to do more? If your spouse showed his or her appreciation for what you do for them and your family, how would you feel? Would you then want to show your appreciation for them?

Appreciation is a skill that must be learned especially if this is not a part of your normal way of interacting with people. Teachers call it, catching the child doing something good. This is the same concept, we want you to learn. Catch your spouse doing something good and then praise them for it, especially if it is something that you have asked them to improve.

Appreciation can come in the form of physical and verbal appreciation. You can appreciate or give your spouse praise for something they have said or done. They could've supported you on a project that you knew took a lot for them to get behind you on or they could have decided to spend time with some people they really didn't like because they knew it was important to you. Appreciation is your way of showing your spouse that you appreciate the blessing that God has given to you by giving you your spouse, showing thankfulness and gratitude even for the small things that they do. Once you begin to focus on the positive, the less energy it will take to catch them doing something good. The thing that you shine a light on is the thing that is magnified. Shine a light on the positive side of your relationship. No that does not diminish that fact that there are some things that may be going wrong in your relationship, but it does help you deal with the negative in a better way when you have created a positive well to draw from.

Many couples have learned to appreciate their spouse much more because they have been brought through a struggle. God does not take you around or over struggle; he brings you through the struggle so that you and your relationship with Him and your spouse can be greater. Learning to appreciate this process and then the outcome helps you have a much better perspective while you're going through the struggle. We know while you're in it, this focus on the positive outcome is easier said than done. However, we all have examples of times when we were able to overcome some sort of struggle and can attest to how much stronger we were for having gone through it. The same concept applies to your relationship. You have to trust that being able to make it through your struggle can make your relationship stronger and draw you even closer. While going through whatever struggle you are having large or small, you have to be mindful of how you treat one another. Criticizing, pointing out flaws, attacking, finding fault or focusing on what is wrong is a sure ticket to maintaining your stay in the struggle. As opposed to being thankful for the struggle, being appreciative of growth, and offering praise which can move you through the struggle much quicker.

Sometimes, in an effort to make things better, we create our own monsters, as we said in Chapter 4. For example, early on in our marriage, I would criticize how my wife did things. In her mind after so much of this, she felt like I was judging her, which made her feel less than and not good enough. After a while, she just gave up because she felt like no matter what she did, she was wrong. Who wants to be wrong all the time? Instead of pointing out what I felt was wrong all the time, I should have shown my appreciation when she did do something I liked. There were many missed opportunities when she did something I liked, but I didn't focus on that. I continued to focus on what she didn't do. After I realized that she responded much better to my appreciation rather than my criticism, I changed the way I spoke to her and treated her. When I began to simply say, thank you and then specifically point out what it was I appreciated, I began to see a change in her attitude and behavior towards me and the things I had asked her to do.

Men you really need to try this, it really does work. At first it may seem a little artificial, but eventually it will become a habit. Ladies, it doesn't have to be anything big, it could be something as small as your husband remembered to take out the trash and you didn't have to remind him or in his mind "nag" him. If he does this, thank him and specifically state what you appreciate without any criticism or sarcasm attached. You may be saying to yourself that is something he is supposed to do anyway, why should I thank him? How do you feel at work when you do something large or small and it goes unnoticed? After a while you begin to feel like you're being taken for granted and eventually you could start thinking to yourself, these people don't appreciate me and all my hard work, I'm going to look for a job where someone does appreciate me. Could this be what your spouse is feeling? Do you want them to look elsewhere to be appreciated? Wouldn't you like some recognition and appreciation for your efforts.... well so would your spouse. Often times the very thing that we are looking for in our relationships is the same thing that our spouse is looking for, we are just saying it in different ways.

We can't tell you how many times couples have come to see us for counseling and the husband and wife are venting about what they see as the issue in their marriage and when you peel away the top surface areas, they are asking for the same needs to be met. It's funny how when you become so focused on what you are not getting, you lose sight of what you are getting and it can cloud your judgment as to what you are doing to meet that same need in your spouse. We will talk in chapter 8 about how a reciprocal relationship is necessary to keep the love flowing from one spouse to the other.

Reciprocity is a key in many of the tenets in this book and appreciation is no different. Showing appreciation to one another can create a cycle of appreciation that continues to flow, but someone has to start. Will it be you?

One area that continues to come up when a couple is learning this concept of appreciation and catching their spouse doing good, is one or both of the spouses have a hard time with this because they have not learned to appreciate themselves. That's something to think about. If you come from a home where praise was not given and criticism or fault finding was the order of the day, it is a lot harder for that person to learn to look at the good in their spouse. This person came from a home that may have had a lot of arguing and yelling and maybe even some abuse. If this is the history of what you have learned it is hard to then go to, honey I really do appreciate you when... This person has to work much harder to focus on what their spouse is doing right because they are used to looking at life and others through a critical eye, including themselves.

Are you this type of person? Are you overly critical of yourself, your spouse, or your children? What are some things that you have found fault within yourself? Take a sheet of paper and number them and write them out. How many do you have? How do you feel under the weight of your own criticism? Not so good huh. How do you think your spouse or your children feel under your weight of criticism? Now look back at your paper and see the negative things that you have written about yourself, for each one that you have written, I want you to write something that you appreciate about yourself to counteract them. So for example if you have 5 negative things you criticize yourself for then you need 5 things that you appreciate about yourself. Even if you were able to write 100, you need to come up with a positive thing that you appreciate about yourself to counteract that negative. If this assignment does not apply to you, then take this same assignment and write all of the criticisms that you have about your spouse and number them. Then write next to them the things that you appreciate. See the chart below. If you need more space you can use the samples in the appendix.

Criticism	Appreciation

Criticism / Appreciation List Figure 5.1

Once you learn to appreciate your spouse, you learn to look for the simplest things about them that you like or admire. This leads to a deeper level of affection and respect. All men want to feel respected as a man, for who they are and who they are called to be for you. All women want to be respected as a woman not mistreated or taken for granted and shown that you appreciate them through the ways that she would like to be appreciated. So if your wife likes flowers, it's okay to show her that you appreciate her through flowers. If your husband likes electronic gadgets, it's okay to give him a just because gift.

Appreciation can be shown through words, actions, tangible items such as gifts and through uninterrupted focused attention on your spouse. Some words of appreciation are, thank you, I appreciate you, you are the best, God knew what he was doing when he made you, I admire you, I thank God for you, I am blessed to have you. Of course, gifts are whatever your spouse would appreciate, so if your spouse likes cards, then buy a card. If your spouse likes massages then buy her a massage. If your husband likes golf then buy him a round at the golf course. This is where being attentive to your spouse's needs come in.

Uninterrupted focused time and attention means just that, no TV, cell phones, video games, work, friends, family or children. This type of time can make the world of a difference in a relationship. Sometimes, we get so busy with life that we forget that we have a spouse that needs just as much attention if not more than all the other things that we tend to give attention to. Sometimes, however, in order to give that uninterrupted focused time, there may be some sacrifice. What if your wife had a really rough day at work and you noticed at dinner she was just a little more distant than usual. You asked her what's wrong, but all she said was, rough day and got a little glassy eyed. She didn't cry because the children were at the table, but you could tell she was really upset. Now dinner is over and after a lot of silence, she begins to prepare the children for bed. You check the TV listing because you know there is a big playoff game tonight, as you are doing this you catch a glimpse of your wife and she still hasn't snapped out of it. What do you do at this moment? Do you say to yourself, ahh she'll get over it, this isn't the first time she has had a bad day, besides, the game is about to come on? Or, do you say, I better go check on her because she seems a little more upset than usual?

Now as you're processing this in your head, what if you did this last scenario? You go to your wife and begin to tell her how much you appreciate her for all of the effort she makes to go to a job that you know that she is not happy with because she is working to move your family forward. You then ask her to tell you about her day and what was so upsetting. While she is talking, you are fully engaged not distracted by the game or even the thought of the game because you want to make sure she can feel that you are giving her your undivided attention. Once she's done, you hug her and hold on to her, tell her you love her and that you want to take care of her just like she has taken care of you and your family. You could go one step further, because you know your wife likes baths, you go run her some bath water with the scented candles and pour her favorite drink. You then tell her that she should relax in the tub and allow you to take care of her for the rest of the night with whatever she needs.

As you can see appreciation comes in all forms in this last scenario including sacrifice, because you would have missed some if not all of the game to make sure you show your wife how much you love and appreciate her. After this, how do you think your wife would feel? Do you think she would feel loved and appreciated? Do you think she would feel this appreciation at a deeper level? Do you think she would feel closer to you and would be more willing to show the same kind of appreciation towards you? Now we know what most brothers are thinking, I know if I do all of that, we are definitely going to have sex. Ahh yes, we know you so well. However, don't let that be your motivation and don't allow yourself to be angry if it doesn't happen because remember you did all of that to show her your appreciation towards her. Of course, if it does happen, that's a definite bonus and you should then tell her you appreciate her for making love with you even after such a rough day.

Appreciation is thoughtfulness, paying attention to your spouse's needs and then doing your best to meet those needs. Even as we are writing this book my husband, Ben took the time to show how much he appreciated me as the mother of his children by pampering me with things that he knew that I would enjoy and appreciate and in return I thanked him for taking such good care of me and our children. Appreciation as we said is reciprocal, if your spouse does or says something in appreciation to you, you must then show your appreciation towards them and the cycle continues.

As a way for you to notice the positive things that your spouse has done, for the next 21 days we want you to write down everything that you appreciate about your spouse. When you notice them doing something no matter how big or small write it down and show your appreciation for it. For example, your wife picked up your socks that you left on the floor of the bedroom. Your husband let you watch the program that you wanted to watch even though there was a football game on and after 21 days, review what you have written and up the ante! Challenge yourself to continue to do this project until it no longer feels like a project and you are actively doing this on your own, when it is no longer artificial. Challenge yourself even in the face of discouragement to continue.

Ladies, let me tell you a little secret about men. We need to feel like you want us around. We are problem solvers by nature and we need to feel important to you. Ladies, men need to feel appreciated and we need to feel that we mean something to you. We LOVE to hear that we are doing a great job, we even like to hear that we aren't doing such a great job, however it's not in what is said, it's how you say it. We are truly competitive by nature, so anything to help us rise to the top of our "A" game, we are all in. Nothing makes a man walk like a proud peacock, with all his feathers spread out wide and colorful more than the words of appreciation and love from his woman. When a man is shown appreciation for the little things even though you think that it's his responsibility and you shouldn't have to, you can get the world from him. For example, if he helps around the house with the household duties like washing clothes, cleaning the kitchen or even doing the girls' hair. (Yes brothers, I do my daughters hair, and we have four of them.) When my wife shows me appreciation by simply saying thank you, it makes me want to do more for her, to help take the load off of her shoulders. Appreciation is a natural human response when someone acknowledges what you have done for them. Basically, a few simple words of inspiration and encouragement can go a long way. When you give kind words and words of appreciation, you speak like into the spirit of the person receiving it. When was the last time you did something for someone and they did **not** show appreciation for what you took time and energy to do? How did you feel?

Words of appreciation for something that someone else has done knowingly or unknowingly for you warrant your acknowledgement. What happens when you don't give those words of appreciation, you wind up opening up the door for outside influences to speak life into your husband or wife.

What do we mean, we're glad you asked. Co-workers acknowledged what a great job you did on your presentation and your wife or husband watched you tirelessly for 4 nights straight getting that presentation together and not once said how proud they were of you pushing through that project to make it right so that you could get that promotion and help provide more for the needs of the family. You see everything has a cause and effect, just in this example you see how the co-worker was given a pass into the heart of your spouse by you from not being attentive to their needs. It is easy to take your spouse for granted because you see them every day and sometimes we believe certain things should be done without recognition, but if this would help to encourage your spouse, what is wrong with it?

We know some people are thinking they don't show their appreciation for me. That may be true, but someone has to start the process of repairing, restoring or revitalizing your relationship. We all play a role in our relationships whether it is an active or a passive one. You can passively stand by and watch your relationship deteriorate or you can actively pursue change. Focus on the positive in your relationship. Acknowledge what your spouse does well; catch your spouse doing good. Praise your spouse for the good that they do in your relationship and for every negative thought, attribute or statement you've made about your spouse, replace it with an appreciation.

Applications Questions:

1. What can you do to show your spouse that you appreciate them?

2. How do you think your spouse would feel if you "caught them being good" and showed your appreciation for whatever they have said or done?

3. Is there something that you may have taken your spouse for granted about? If so, how can you show them that you appreciate them now?

Be willing to:

1. Appreciate your spouse for who they are.

2. Appreciate your spouse for what they do; even the little things.

3. Appreciate your spouse in verbal and non-verbal ways.

4. Replace the negative attributes you have given your spouse with the things that you appreciate about them.

5. Encourage your spouse by acknowledging and then praising them for the things that they are doing to meet your needs.

6. Actively pursue positive change in your relationship.

Ask God:

To help you recognize the good in your spouse and remove the criticism that you have for your spouse or even for yourself. Ask him to allow you to love your spouse unconditionally and appreciate them. Finally ask him to help you to not take your spouse for granted and convict you when you are.

CHAPTER SIX

Friendship

Are you friends with your spouse? If you are, what does that friendship look like? Would you say that your spouse is your best friend? Are other friendships more important than the friendship with your spouse? Why do you think that is? Do other friendships meet the needs that your spouse doesn't?

During the dating phase, you learned your spouse's ways. You did whatever it took to make them happy. If they liked time, you spent time with them. If they liked gifts, you gave them gifts. If they liked home cooked meals, you cooked for them. If they liked phone calls, texts, emails, facebook, twitter, etc. you did that too. If they liked physical affection, you showed your affection physically. What happened to all of that? You moved from dating to marriage and it changed, but the expectation for all of that still remains. There is now an expectation of the need for friendship being met, but it has changed or is no longer there. The lack of the need being met can lead to disillusion, jealousy, anger and even resentment.

These are some strong feelings that are hard to come back from because they can become so entrenched that you don't even realize it. These feelings can lead to the outward expression of them and you don't know where they came from. For example, your spouse has said, I want us to spend some time together, we haven't been alone in weeks. You say, I can't I'm busy with children, school, work, church, mom, dad, my friend mike, basketball, golf, anything other than you. How do you think your spouse feels? How would you feel if you were the one being turned down? Rejected.

Rejection is a strong feeling and after a while the person who is getting rejected will just give up, because no one wants to get rejected over and over again. Then the resentment sets in for the thing or the person that has replaced the time that should have been spent with you because you feel like that person or that thing is more important than you. Now every time you say you are going to go play basketball, hang out with your friend Mike, take on another class, finish up some work until late at night, go to another program or meeting at the church, take your child out or let the child sleep in your bed another night, your husband or wife seems to get an attitude. What person or thing has replaced your spouse? Had you even realized that you made that thing more important to you than your spouse? Did you realize that there was some jealousy and resentment there?

Often when we talk to couples in our groups and in couple's sessions, this issue will come up. The problem is, each person is so focused on what the other person is **not doing** that they don't take the time to see that, hey, maybe I'm not doing my part either. How many times have you said to yourself, ladies, well he hasn't taken me out on a date in months, so I'm not going to ….? Or men, how many times have you said to yourself, she doesn't want to go to the gym with me anymore and it seems like I have to practically force her, I'm not going to ….?

Friendship is reciprocal, there's that word again. Someone has to start or restart. You can't tell us you don't know where to start. No one had to tell you where to start, you just did it when you were dating. We know you're thinking, if I knew where to start we wouldn't be looking to you for answers. Trust us, you do know where to start, go back to the beginning. The beginning of your relationship is where you start. What was it at that time that your husband or wife liked? What kinds of things did you do or say that they appreciated? If those things are too long ago, then take the time to study your spouse and ask questions? For example, if it has been a while since you have done something with your spouse ask them when was the last time you did something they really enjoyed, then prod them to tell you more. Ask them, if you could describe the perfect date with me, what would that look like? If you were the happiest you had ever been with me, what would I be doing to make that happen? Now some of these may be a little harder for them to answer because they may not have ever thought about it, so be ready for that answer. Give them time to think about it, but let them know that you will be coming back for an answer because it is really important to you. You need to be ready with your answers to those questions as well. Don't be afraid to ask questions and then act on the answers. Be bold.

Your wife may like to get her nails and hair done and this is something that she normally does with her friends. Maybe the two of you could go get a massage together or maybe just a pedicure. (We bet if you do, your wife will see this as romantic and it could lead to the eros love we will discuss later…. wink, wink. But don't let this be your sole motivation because your wife will see right through you, there is no guarantee that This will lead to That.) Ladies why not try getting some tickets to the local high school basketball game or to the professional sports team in town and take your man to see the game. Friendship is sometimes about doing things that you may not want to, but you know that your spouse will enjoy it. Friendship is also about finding that middle ground around something that you both can enjoy. Friendship is the way to rekindle a relationship whose flame has died out.

Men let me let you in on a little secret; women like to feel like they are important in your life and that you actually took the time to think about them. Whether that means picking up a card on the way home that says thank you for the great job you do with the kids, or you cooking dinner on a Sunday afternoon just because, or treating her to a spa day, or buying her that piece of jewelry that she has been eyeing. As you can see I really like the spa. Friendship is an opportunity to get to know your spouse on a level that most people never will. You have the opportunity to ask them questions about things that are personal to them and close to their heart to show your interest in them. Why not sit down with your spouse and really connect with them. Find out what is going on with them. Maybe they have been really struggling with something but haven't talked to you about it because you have been so distant or just busy lately.

We see friendship as an integral part of any marriage and the lack of it can destroy a marriage. Don't ever underestimate the power of friendship in a relationship, if left untreated, this area is the area that can lead to divorce and or an affair. Have you seen those couples who have been married for 18, 20, even 35 years get a divorce? Among the rubble of their destroyed relationship, almost always you'll find the lack of friendship there. Why is that? In most instances these people are getting a divorce after the children are gone, a business has failed, they have hit retirement. All of the things that used to occupy their time and help them mask their lack of friendship are gone. Now the reality that they are living with someone they really don't know is staring them in the face.

Maybe you've seen this scenario, It starts with an innocent cup of coffee before work, or going for lunch with a group of coworkers but the husband and his female coworker just happen to start talking and they decide to go have lunch together next week with just the two of them. Well next week comes, they have the lunch and have a really good time and they realize that they hit it off, nothing sexual; they just have a good time together. Well instead of telling his wife what happened that day he texts her during the day back and forth about the office politics. The husband and wife's friendship is being taken by someone else because either the wife is too busy, too distant, or too irritated by him to realize that their friendship has eroded and before she knows it, she is no longer his friend; someone else is. Someone else has taken that space and now he's coming to tell his wife about his new friend who listens when she doesn't, who takes the time to hear him out and doesn't talk over him or treats him like one of the kids.

Don't get us wrong here, this last scenario could have just as easily been the wife seeking friendship outside of the relationship. In fact, most of the time when there has been an infidelity where the wife is the culprit, this is usually how it has started. However, both scenarios could be a whole lot different if they would have taken the time to cultivate their friendship.

In the law of sowing and reaping, we understand, basically that we reap what we sow. If you sow nothing, you reap nothing. If you sow a little, you reap a little. In other words, if you only put in little to no effort in your friendship / relationship, then you are going to get little to no effort from your spouse.

A friendship is like a flower that you are trying to grow, you have to water it, feed it and make sure it has sunlight, and it has to be nourished. Are you nourishing your friendship with your spouse with kind words and deeds, or are you killing it through starvation (lack of time) and berating it in an outwardly verbal way or even to yourself? The mind is a powerful tool. Even if you are saying all of the right things, what are you thinking? Are you thinking, this isn't going to work or he or she won't appreciate what I'm doing anyway? I'll try this just to make sure I've done all that I can do, but I know this won't work? You reap what you sow.

The law of attraction says if you put out negativity, that is what you receive in return, but if you put out positivity, that is what you'll receive. Relationships can go through phases of ups and downs. The downs are sometimes just a rut that doesn't have to take that long. Tell it to get the rut out of here. You determine how long the rut is. It can last a few weeks, a few months or even years. Make the choice to make a change today!

Let's talk a moment about friendship with other people. Now we are all for you keeping friendships and even making new ones, however, if those friends can't be OUR friends, then they are not your friend. What we mean by that is, if that person who is your friend is not a friend of your marriage and the success of it, then they should not be your friend. If that person is someone you would not be friends with if your spouse was aware of it, then they should not be your friend.

Friends to your marriage are people who will support your marriage as a whole with all of the ups and downs. Your marriage doesn't need people who are going to add fuel to the fire or who will talk in your ear about how it isn't working so you should move on. True friends tell you the truth, encourage you and even confront you. They hold you accountable without having disparaging remarks about your spouse. If they are speaking negatively about your spouse, then that is where you have to place some boundaries around your relationship and stand up for your spouse even if you think they're right.

Marriage is a funny thing. It takes a lot of work as you can see, so why would you allow someone else to destroy all of the hard work that you have put in by talking down about your relationship? If you are trying your best to be as positive about your relationship as possible, don't allow other people's negative thoughts and comments to come in and cloud your judgment, even if that person is your mom or your dad. We know that's a rough one, but the bible does talk about a man should leave his mother and his father and cleave to his wife. This means you are to leave all others so that your spouse can be first and all those others should be left out of your relationships. Have you heard the saying, when you get married, you should keep everybody out of your business? Why do you think people say that? Because time and time again someone has allowed a family member or a friend in on their relationship business and that friend or family member was not supportive of their marital relationship and said or did some things to tear it down.

Friendship is an integral part of the marital relationship. It is a part of the three part triumvirate. It is a part of the three types of love in the Greek language, which are eros, philia and agape love. Eros is the sensual love, philia is the friendship part of a relationship and agape is the unselfish, unconditional love in a marital relationship. We need all three to make our marriages successful. If one is off kilter then the other two are likely out of whack as well. Don't take your friendship with your spouse for granted.

Men, my wife is my homey, my peoples, my confidant, and my ear. I have so much fun with her. There have been many nights we have laid in bed after putting the girls down for the night and wondered what the girls thought of us because we would be laughing and talking so loudly about ... whatever. Most of the time, my wife would say, "I think they think that we are crazy" and "what is so funny". It's a great feeling to have someone that you can talk to about anything, and not feel that they will use it against you in a disagreement later.

Ladies please be aware of this. Men don't readily open up and share their inner most feelings for fear of having it thrown up in their face in a disagreement later on or at an inappropriate place or time. When a man does open up to you and shares with you what he has never shared with anyone else he is vulnerable and you must guard that bit of information with your life if you ever want him to open up to you again. Don't violate his trust in you by falling victim to you wanting to be RIGHT.

What I mean by this is, the two of you are having a disagreement and a lot of things have been said but in your eyes he is winning this argument, so for the sake of winning and being right, you blurt out what he shared with you in confidence. Uh oh! You have just shut him down and created a new wall. He may never be that vulnerable with you again or at least until he feels safe enough again to share with you without it being thrown back in his face. Men are naturally guarded because of fear of how society looks at a man who shares his feelings as being weak; so when he opens up his heart, he's comfortable and has let down his guard because you have told him in so many ways that you will never hurt him and you will always be there for him. That's true friendship, when you can share your inner most thoughts with your spouse/friend with the comfort of no backlash from them. I can readily attest to having the comfort of being able to share things with my wife that I thought were sacred to me and never hearing it ever again, unless I gave permission for it to be repeated publicly. You will have many acquaintances in your life however you will only have a hand full of real friends, but one of those 5 needs to be your spouse.

Applications Questions:

1. Do you view your spouse as your friend? Why or Why not?

2. What type of friendship do you and your spouse have?

3. How much time do you two spend cultivating this part of your relationship?

4. What are you willing to do to make your friendship better?

Be willing to:

1. Make your spouse your friend.

2. Find out what things your spouse likes and then enjoy some of them with your spouse.

3. Guard your friendship from others and divorce.

4. Cultivate your friendship by being a friend.

Ask God:

To help you to be a friend to your spouse and make the times that you spend together enjoyable.

SIDE NOTE:

At this point in the book, we realize that if you have been following along and even attempting what we have suggested, you could be feeling a little weary, especially if what you have done has been to no avail. We want to encourage you to keep going with the task that you have set out to do of repairing, restoring or revitalizing your relationship. Stay vigilant and stay prayerful. Pray, Father please give me the strength to not only trust that my spouse and I can make the changes needed in our relationship but that I can trust your promise to me that love never fails. Thank you Father in advance for your mercy and grace and the renewal of our relationship.

CHAPTER SEVEN

Love Never Fails

Do you love your spouse? Are you in love with your spouse? Are you able to show your spouse that you love them no matter what they have said or done? Are you able to love them the way God loves you? Do you think this is possible for your relationship? Does the love you have for your spouse show that you are one? What would happen if you selflessly loved your spouse, expecting nothing in return? How would your relationship change or grow? We call this chapter the unusual kind of love because it goes against the grain, it is not how most people view what love looks like. This love is one that compels you to love the other person even when you don't like them. We all have those days when you don't like that person very much. As you are reading this, today could be that day. Well what do you do with that? With this kind of love, you are called to love them anyway. What a novel concept, at least for some. Many people in this situation, after so many days of not liking the person would say, well, if I'm not happy, I am just going to give up, throw in the towel, talk to some friends about this, seek outside counsel, get a divorce. This unusual kind of love, agape love, NEVER FAILS! Even as we're writing this looking at the words, never fails is a deep concept, one that you have to let sit there for a minute and let it marinate. We know that this is a hard concept especially when so many in our society today say that we should just walk away if we are not happy, feel we are being mistreated, she has let herself go, we are going in separate directions, there are so many reasons. This love takes work, a lot of hard work, a lot of sacrifice and a lot of willingness. Yes willingness, there goes that word again. We keep bringing it up because it is crucial that even if you don't feel like you love that person today or even like them, that you are at least willing to seek out why and then be willing to make the necessary changes.

The unusual kind of love is an abiding love. A love where you must spend time with each other learning and growing together like the abiding relationship with God. The more time you spend with Him, helps you desire to spend more time with your spouse. Remember when you were first dating, you spent so much time together… you couldn't get enough of each other. You wanted to spend every waking moment with each other. You spent hours and hours on the phone talking about … nothing. What was different about your spouse then? True, they may have changed some but so have you. At the core, they are still the person you married. What can you do to get back to that place? Spend time together. Get to know them again. Study them like you did before. Begin to understand them for who they are now and not just for who they were when you married them. This unusual love is patient, kind, not jealous, is not rude, is not selfish, doesn't insist on its own way, not easily angered, doesn't keep score, rejoices in the truth, is not arrogant, doesn't brag, and never fails. It bears all things, believes all things, hopes all things and endures all things. It is compassionate, humble, gentle, bearing with one another, forgiving one another. (Scripture reference I Corinthians 13:4-7)

There are three cornerstones that we believe create agape love, which are becoming one, loving one another as Christ loved the church and forgiveness. We will cover two of the cornerstones in this chapter, becoming one and loving as Christ loved the church, but we will cover forgiveness in a separate chapter.

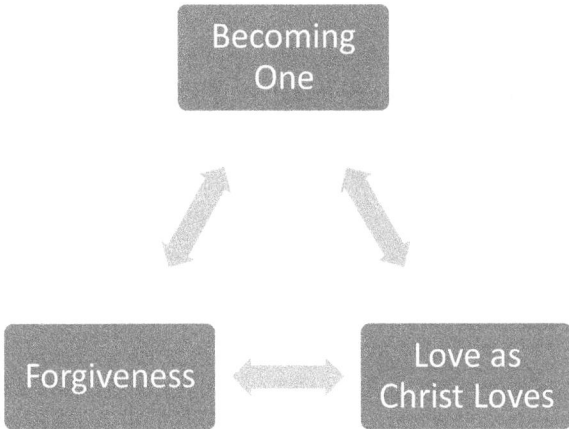

Three Cornerstones of Agape Love, Figure 7.1

BECOMING ONE

We absolutely need God for this type of love. He is the third cord in the three-stranded cord. A three-stranded cord is not easily broken. Even when the sides are worn down the middle portion of the cord is still holding on and keeping the two together. Is God at the center of your relationship? If He is not, who or what is? Is it your friends, your mom, dad, siblings, your children, your job, material things, maybe its depression, selfishness? What about another woman or another man, porn, or maybe it's you? There are so many things that could have been placed in the middle of your relationship and have caused a barrier to you loving one another. Whatever it is, it must be removed. What happens when you break your arm? It hurts, you bleed, it's extremely painful and it takes time to heal. Unless the broken arm is set right, it will never be the same. This is similar to what happens in marriages, there is a break that's painful and hurts and if it isn't set right there can be a decline in the marriage and eventually end in divorce.

The way God intended marriage was for a man and a woman to become one as in Genesis 2:23-24. When Adam says, this is now bone of my bones and flesh of my flesh: she shall be called woman because she was taken out of man. Therefore, shall a man leave his father and his mother and shall cleave unto his wife, and they shall be one flesh. When two become one in a marriage, you fit with one another. You bring the good out of one another. You bring different perspectives to the same issue that helps get the issues resolved. Now becoming one is no easy task, in fact we call it a beast, because it is a really hard process, and it is a process. We have to work daily to make this happen. Becoming one entails every aspect of your life with your spouse: physically, emotionally, mentally, spiritually, and financially. You know the saying, "we can finish each other's sentences"? This is a true statement when the two are one, when the two are becoming like-minded. Just as you have to work to become one daily, you have to work consistently to keep the barriers to becoming one out of your relationship.

What are some of the barriers to you becoming one with your spouse physically? What's keeping you from being intimate with your spouse? What's keeping you from regularly enjoying sexual pleasure with your spouse? Are there some past hurts or disappointments that are keeping you from fully connecting with your spouse? What's keeping you from mentally connecting with your spouse? Do you have issues of trust with them, their decision-making process, their way of thinking, or whether they make decisions based on what's best for them or the whole family. What's keeping you from becoming one with your spouse financially? Oh yes we said it! So many people will connect in every other way, but refuse to commit financially. What's keeping you from doing this? Some of the barriers that can play out for couples can be barriers as it relates to beliefs/values, friends, family, time (the amount of time you do or don't invest in your relationship), lack of intimacy, lack of sex, lack of feelings of love, trust, compassion, negative feelings towards your spouse, and proximity to one another. Sometimes, sheer physical distance can cause a barrier to becoming one. Being unwilling. As you've noticed at the end of each chapter, we talk about ways you can apply what we've written by being willing to do the things we've requested, well if you are not even willing to look at the possibility that you need to make some changes then even that can be your barrier to becoming one.

Some other barriers to becoming one:

Family and friends either bringing their thoughts and ideas about how a marriage should work that goes against what you and your spouse are trying to create. Family and friends having hurt feelings because you are now investing more time in your spouse than in the relationship with them.

Past experiences – Maybe you've never seen a successful marriage where the two people really do enjoy one another and work hard on "becoming one". It's hard to visualize something when you have no frame of reference, no way to even see how that works.

Expectations- We will discuss this further in the next chapter, but expectations can be a huge barrier to becoming one. You need to voice what you expect or need from your spouse effectively so that you can have your deepest needs the way you feel loved met. Without having your needs met, resentment, lack of trust even anger sets in and all of these obviously are barriers to loving your spouse and becoming one.

Having a framework of independence even in your marriage and not interdependence or thinking and feeling that you can think and act independently of your spouse without it having any ramifications on your relationship or your spouse, can be a barrier to becoming one. We see this a lot from women, they don't want to let their guard down because they've been hurt or momma or grandmomma told them to make sure you can take care of yourself and never depend on a man. Yes, you should know how to take care of yourself, but you should also be able to enjoy being taken care of. Don't be threatened by the care and love that Christ has for you through the flesh of your husband. God wants to use your spouse as a living, breathing manifestation of His love for you.

Let me speak to the ladies for a minute. Why do you feel like you don't deserve or are not worthy of this kind of love, the kind of love where a man would lay down his life for you? Often times we get in our own way when it comes to the love we seek. We say we want a man who can love us unconditionally, who we can trust will take care of us for richer or poorer, in sickness and in health but when we find him we say "he's too nice", or we choose the one we know is not right for us. We have to learn to accept this kind of love, if not we are creating the self-fulfilling prophecy that no man can take care of me, love me, or is good enough. So when he doesn't meet this expectation, that you fully expected that he wouldn't, you get mad at him for setting him up to fail. We are setting up the boundaries, walls, limitations, that won't allow these men, our men, your man to love you. What barriers have you put in place to becoming one?

Men we're not letting you off the hook. In this area often times men set up the barrier where they misrepresent what it means to love their wives. Men are to love their wives as Christ loved the church. Christ loved the church selflessly not selfishly. He laid down His life for his bride (the church). He didn't belittle her, talk down to her, bang his chest and say, "I'm the head of this house, so you should follow what I say". He wasn't a dictator, he was a servant-leader. He led by example. Maybe your wife is having a hard time becoming one with you because of your example.

When you become one bear all things that your spouse brings to the table, what life throws at you and continue to love one another through it. This means if your spouse comes to the marriage with issues with depression, you love them through it. There is job loss during the marriage, you love them through it. Someone becomes ill, you love them through it. You have a sick child or maybe you even lose a child, you love them through it. You carry them when they can't. You bear one another's burdens. You bear all things together so the load for one doesn't become too heavy.

You don't lose hope. You continue to have hope in your relationship in your spouse and in your future together. One of the worst things you can do to a man is to lose hope in him. A married man whose wife no longer believes in him is a dejected and angry man. Wives you have to be your husband's number one cheerleader, encouraging and not discouraging him. If a man's wife believes in him, he believes he can accomplish anything. Men your wives need to know that you don't take her for granted or feel like an issue won't be resolved because it has always been that way. Never lose hope in your spouse and in your marriage.

Love never fails. This part of the passage makes a strong statement. It comes after all of the other statements that really could be barriers to the love that the two of you share. Then it says love never fails. It's like the bible is saying, I know all these things can and will occur, but love never fails. I know there will be times when you may feel jealous, but love never fails. There may be times where you may lose patience, but love never fails. He may be irritating you to no end but love never fails. Even though you felt like your wife is being rude and has been for the last few months, love never fails. Your husband has been selfish in making decisions based on what's best for him and not the family, but love never fails. You both can have a quick temper and sometimes conversations escalate and things get out of hand, but love never fails. There have been 15 times in the last year you have asked your wife to spend time with you without the interference of friends, baby, work, but love never fails. You feel like your spouse is not supportive of you and your dreams, but love never fails. There are times you can't trust them because of hints of infidelity or even pornography, but love never fails. Look again at I Corinthians 13:4-7 through the context of your relationship and see how your issues fit within those few chapters. God has known even before you and your spouse were born that you would have issues. He knew that the two of you would have barriers to the type of love he has set forth for you, that is why He has given you the blueprint to make your marriage work. There will always be ups and downs in a marriage, but God has given you a simple tool to judge whether or not the love for your spouse is meeting the standard that He has set forth and that is I Corinthians 13:4-7. Ask yourself is the way you love your spouse represented by all of these attributes, if not why and what do you need to change to make sure that you do? No we are definitely not saying that you will display this type of love at all times, but you know when you are not and it is your responsibility to make the necessary changes. Don't wait for your spouse to make the changes necessary first. You make them. Ultimately, your displaying this type of love really is not just to your spouse, you are also showing your love for God by loving your spouse in this way. You are showing God that you honor the covenant that was made with Him and your spouse. Marriage under this kind of love is a covenant and not a contract. By honoring and loving your spouse, you are honoring and loving God.

Because God really does want you to succeed, He gives us tools to help in the areas that we may consider difficult. The following area of loving your spouse like Christ loved the church is difficult with the tools he provides and His guidance. The second cornerstone of agape love is loving your spouse as Christ loves the church.

Love as Christ Loves

Loving as Christ loves can feel unnatural if we go by the world's standards. People who have never seen or experienced this will tell you that this kind of love is impossible. They will say that there is no way you can love someone like this. Well this is one of those times where you have to ask yourself, what do I believe? Do I believe what the bible says or do I believe what "they" say?

Agape love is the kind of love that feels so good that when you find it, you spiritually connect to it because you feel a relief, a sense of I belong here. You want to luxuriate there and enjoy it. The bible speaks of this love in Ephesians 5:21-33. Men love to quote this area in the bible because it talks about submission. Yes we'll get to that, but before we do, in the verses Ephesians 5:25-29, the bible says: 25Husbands love your wives, just as Christ also loved the church and gave Himself for her,26 that He might sanctify and cleanse her with the washing of water by the word, 27 that He might present her to Himself a glorious church, not having spot or wrinkle or any such thing, but that she should be holy and without blemish.28 So husbands ought to love their own wives as their own bodies; he who loves his wife loves himself.29 For no one ever hated his own flesh, but nourishes and cherishes it, just as the Lord does the church.

When you think about how Christ loves the church, what do you think of? Well when we think about it, we think about something sweet, innocent, pure. We think about strength, courage, selflessness, care, concern and sacrifice. We think about a love so deep that we can hardly fathom it. A love so deep that it touches the core of our souls. It is so deep that just the thought makes us ask, what did we do to deserve this kind of unconditional love? A love that loves you even when you are unlovable, loves you even when you are wrong. A love that doesn't keep score or keep a mark on my record. You are forgiven. Wow, what would you give to be loved like that? Are you loved like that by anyone? Do you love anyone like that? What if you loved your wife like that? What if you felt this kind of love from your husband?

Jesus presented His bride without spot or wrinkle, that means when he talked about her to others, it was never in a negative light. He always saw her in the perfect light even though she had flaws. He only wanted what was best for her and every decision he made was made with her best interest even when it was to his detriment. He loves her, he cherishes her, he nourishes her.

He cherished her by loving her the way no one else could. He showed his loved by providing for her, protecting her, leading her and tending to her faults to make her better. He nourished her by first nourishing himself. He took care of himself physically, emotionally and spiritually and by doing so, he led by example. Husbands, how are you nourishing and cherishing your wife? How are you meeting her needs that are at her core, not just the ones on the surface? How are you tapping into the essence of who she truly is?

What are some of the ways your wife has told you that she likes to be loved? Does she like it when you tell her how much you love her, tell her how much you appreciate her or thank her for what she has done? Does she like it when you spend time with her giving her your undivided attention? Does she like it when the two of you go on dates? Does she like it when you help around the house, when you take on chores? Does she like it when you help with the children and take some responsibility with them? Does she like it when you give her things; cards, flowers, jewelry? Does she like it when you cuddle with her, caress her, kiss her, make love to her? What is it that your wife likes that makes her feel loved? When your woman feels truly loved, you touch her at her core. You lift a weight off of her shoulders, she can walk lighter because she feels taken care of.

At a woman's core, she wants to feel loved, respected, not taken for granted, taken care of, and feel like you are committed to her and your family. She wants to feel that she is number one above anyone or anything else. She wants to feel like she can trust you no matter what and that you will take care of her heart. She wants you to show her that you love her and that you above anyone else you have her back. She wants to know that you consider her in all that you do and that the thought of how this will affect her and your family comes first. She wants you to be thoughtful, if you know she likes a call during the day to see how she's doing, call her. Think about the things that she likes and do it. If you're not sure or maybe you've gotten a little rusty in this department, ask your wife today, what can I do to show you that I love you? Women don't assume that your spouse should or already knows.

Women men need to be loved too. They need to feel that their core needs are met too. Men need to feel respected. They want to feel like their wives honor them and respect them and the decisions they make. It is extremely important to men to feel like you have their back no matter what decision they make , good, bad, and ugly. Men's deepest desires are to have a woman who admires him and will show him and tell him. Men also want to know that you can keep order in the home. They need to feel a sense of peace in the home with order, so if your home is in shambles there will be conflict in your home. In the expectations chapter, we go a little deeper into this and ways that you can discuss one another's needs, but order is a top priority for most men, even if they aren't so orderly. Men want to feel like they can spend time with you, doing things together or at least you watching them participate in activities. You could either find activities that he likes that you can both participate in like softball, tennis, golf or just watch it with them or them participating in it. Men love it when you show them physical affection, men want to be sexual. They want to connect with you physically that is how men give and receive love, this is when men feel bonded. Finally men want to feel like you take them into account with the way you take care of yourself. They want to feel like you still want to make yourself attractive to them. They want to feel like you still take the time to make sure they notice you. They want a wife who is attractive to them.

Men are visual and want to be attracted to the woman they married not look up some years later and feel like they don't know who this woman is in their bed because she looks nothing like the woman he married. I know this is a sticky issue for a lot of women because they feel like a man should love me no matter what, but is that really fair? Take an inventory and make yourself attractive for your spouse.

Servant Leader

To love your wife this way, the way Christ loves the church, you have to be a servant leader. In Matthew 20:28 the bible says, the Son of Man did not come to be served, but to serve... so if you are loving your wife as Christ loved the church, you are to be a servant leader just as he is.

This is the model that was left for men to follow in the role of leader of their homes. We have often times misconstrued what being a leader or head of house looks like. We have taken it to mean, ruler, dictator, boss. What if you were a leader in your home like the example that Jesus left? What if you were a servant leader? What if instead of complaining of what needed to be done, you lead by example?

Many of you may be saying I do that already. Are you sure? What if we took a poll of the people that you are leading? Would they be so assured that you were leading with a servant's heart? When men decide to marry according to what the bible states about marriage, they have decided to humble themselves and become a servant to their wife and to their children. Servant in these terms is someone who meets the needs of the ones who follow them. Servant in these terms does not mean foot stool or hen pecked, but what it does mean is caretaker, provider, nurturer, lover, protector, and priest.

Look at the role that Jesus played. He was a leader. He was a provider. He was a protector. He was a lover of his people. He was a caretaker and a priest. If we are to model our relationships after the one that Christ has with the church, then we have to take in all of what he modeled, not just the parts we like. He was also humble and served even when he knew he would be betrayed. Ok so practically what does that mean? Men we are to serve our wives and our families even in the midst of our anger, hurt, or discontent, even when we feel like she is in the wrong even when our needs aren't being met. I know that feels a little different, because we have been conditioned to only meet the needs of people if they are meeting ours. However, we are to lead by example. If you are leading by being selfish, why then are you surprised if your wife and children are selfish too? Being a servant leader means being humble, leading by example, meeting needs known and unknown, and at times denying your own needs. This is why when we counsel couples, we make it abundantly clear, especially to the men, you carry an awesome responsibility when you choose to be a husband and a father, and if you are not ready for that, walk away before you say I do.

Being a husband and father is an AWESOME at times back-breaking responsibility which is why it must be done in love. Imagine if you had to do the job of husband and father without love in your heart, you would become bitter and resentful. Being bitter and resentful are the quickest ways to harden anyone's heart. Choose to love, protect, provide, take care of, and meet the needs of your wife and family today. Choose to be their servant leader.

Submission

Now let's get to the word that strikes anger in the hearts of some modern, independent women…. submission. I can hear the reactions now from the modern, independent woman; boo, hiss, rolling eyes, why are we even still talking about this. The men are saying, yeah that's right tell 'em, honey are you listening, make sure you take notes.

Submission can be one of those dirty words that has been passed down to be synonymous with slavery, foot stool, fool, weak, not me, you can't make me and if you try, you are in for a fight (at least that is what the women have believed). Men have seen it a little differently. Do as I say do. I am the head of the house and you must follow my rules and if you can't there will be consequences. Some have even taken it as far as becoming physically violent to make their wives submit or mentally and emotionally abusing their wives into submission. Submission doesn't mean beat down 'til you finally give in. These are the meanings that our society has placed on the word submission. Now knowing what you know about how Christ loves us, do you think he would want us to place ourselves in a situation like this? Does this sound like the way Christ loves us, does this line up? No... that's because it doesn't.

God's definition of submission is an act of love. What? Yes, it is an act of love. Submission is done out of love and reverence for the one you are submitting to in marriage. We are referencing Christ's love for the church so often because it is the purest example of this and the ultimate example of what this love looks like. Jesus not only led, but HE submitted. To show us what it should look like, He submitted to the will of God even when he knew he was going to be crucified (Mark 26: 39-42).

Biblically submission or to submit is likened to servant, which in the past has been misconstrued as slave. This is where the backlash has come in with the African American history of enslavement. No one wants to be a slave. To serve someone in the biblical sense is to take care of their needs and to follow them without reprisal. Submission is loving someone enough to trust their judgment, decision-making and their love for you. This area requires a higher level of loving someone.

When the man leads with the authority given him by God in a way that shows that he is a servant leader both he and his spouse are willing and capable of taking on choices and acting responsibly toward one another. The woman will gladly follow where you lead because she is not afraid that you are making moves out of selfish motivation. For example in the beginning of our marriage I would never trust my husband to make a decision for me which meant a decision for the household because I felt that he was always making decisions out of selfish motivations. If he said the sky was blue I said it was black because I felt like he was trying to get over on me or "tell me what to do". In fact one time in an argument I told him, "you can't tell me what to do you ain't my daddy". Of course you know where that led us, to more problems because the more he tried to assert himself the more I fought. The problem was I didn't trust him and ultimately I didn't trust God with the decision to allow this man to be my husband and thus be the head of my house.

Likewise my husband's problem was that he was so busy trying to make me submit and be the dutiful wife that I fought with every ounce of my being. He was not lovingly leading me; he was criticizing and nitpicking his way to get me to do what he wanted. He found fault in everything I did. I could do nothing right. I felt defeated all the time and my hope was gone. I was ready to walk away at a moment's notice. I was digging my way through the Underground Railroad. I was gonna get my freedom. Who knew some years later I would achieve that freedom by staying in the marriage and not walking away? Don't get me wrong, submission is not always easy when your mind goes back to those times when your partner says or did something that you felt was not in your best interest but you have to ask yourself is that is the case now?

Everyone has a position to play just like on a sports franchise team, a quarterback is the head of the offense, without him calling the play and everyone else following his instruction they would just be a bunch of men in a football uniform instead of being a winning team. That's what you should be striving for, a team, with someone who can lead the team to victory. So how do you become a victorious team? We're glad you asked. It starts with the men accepting their roles as head of house and walking in that ordained given purpose. No more excuses, if you didn't have a living example growing up, or your dad was there, but not working in his role in the decision making process ,find a mentor, someone that exudes what you believe to be a good husband/father and become his apprentice. There are plenty of places to seek and find these mighty men of valor, they are in your church, your schools, your fraternal organizations, your boys and girls clubs; they are all around you.

When you surround yourself with Godly men, who can pour into your life and help make you a better man, you help to equip yourself for what is to come. The bible says "iron sharpens iron". As a man, being the head of the house is an awesome responsibility. I tell men all the time in our workshops, that they control the tempo in their homes, whatever good or bad that comes out of their homes is their responsibility . If the kids are acting a fool, it's the man's job to set it straight. If the bills need to be paid, it's the man's role to provide. If there is a lack of spiritual direction in the home, it is the man's role to change that. As you see, these are just the tip of the iceberg when it comes to the responsibilities of a man. Now you can see why many men have abandoned it, it is a lot for one person to take on especially when he hasn't been effectively equipped to do so, but a good leader knows when to call in his winning team for help.

Mutual Submission

Submitting to your spouse means coming under, however, people always skip over verse 21, where the bible speaks of subjecting or submitting yourself one to another. Your submission ultimately is not to your husband, but unto God, you're doing it out of reverence for God. Submission takes a lot of trust, not only in the person you married, but ultimately In God. Submissions says I believe God that I deserve to be loved unconditionally and the person that I married is the walking manifestation of that love.

Submission calls for one to lead and one to follow. God is the head of Christ, Christ is the head of the church and man is the head of his wife; again this is seen from a loving position. For example in every company, there is a one person, a President, who has the final say on the matters of the business and there is a Vice President. Think of it as the husband is the President and the wife is the Vice President. In this example, a truly democratic leader doesn't do this through dictatorship, he does this by taking counsel from his VP. In Genesis 2: , the woman was created as the man's help meet. She was given to be his helper, so decisions although finalized through one person, they are under the counsel of the wife. This is where the trust comes in that the husband is making the best decision selflessly for both and not selfishly for himself.

For example, George an d Lisa are married and they were able to save some money this year, George says he really wants to get a flat screen TV with this money. Lisa says, we don't need a flat screen TV, we've been talking about putting money aside for retirement. In this instance, what decision would be a selfless act? The selfless decision would be to save the money and put it into the retirement account. I know fellas, the flat screen would have looked nice in your bedroom. I love gadgets just as much as the next man. However, this scenario is the perfect opportunity to show leadership for the family as well as how you can submit to your wife and the point she makes of saving money for retirement being a better choice for both of you and not just for you. I know, I know, you're saying she'll get over it because she will eventually enjoy the TV in the bedroom as well. That may be true, but the money saved for retirement meets your wife's deep need for safety and security and it shows that she can trust you. Yeah, everyday choices do count. If you want her to follow you in everything, you have to lead in a way that's best for both of you.

In the beginning, this process can be hard because you are used to making decisions for yourself, but eventually, you will learn to filter choices that can be made for the benefit of both and sometimes the choice will only benefit your mate, but that is what agape love looks like. Agape love is the kind of love that the more you give it, the more it's given to you, the more you want to give it. It becomes a cycle of love instead of the vicious cycle of anger that other couples go through of you did me wrong, so I'll pay you back by doing you wrong. Think of this as the cycle of love.

I love
you

You
love me

I love
you

You
love me

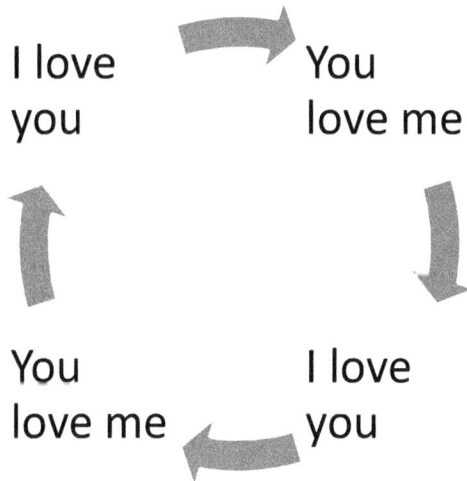

Love Cycle Figure 7.2

Discipleship

Loving as Christ loves really means that you are discipling one another. You are looking to help your spouse become more like Christ. You are not only trying to help them be more like Christ, you are modeling this behavior. You are showing them what Christ's love looks like on a daily basis and are willing to have them help shape you into His image. There is no other person who knows you this way. Your spouse should know every nook and cranny of you emotionally, mentally, physically and spiritually. They should know your dreams as well as your deepest fears. They should know you so well that if someone came to you and said they saw your spouse with another man or woman in a compromising position, they should know whether or not that statement is true and be able to refute it.

If your spouse knows you so well, then they should also be able to help you grow because they have a different vantage point of the direction you are going. They see and feel when you are connected to God and when you are not. They see if you are truly walking the walk that you claim to other people. If all of this is true then they should be able to help make you the best person you can be from pure and not selfish motives. When done correctly, even correction by your spouse feels like love. You might not like it, but if done in love, you feel it. Remember your relationship resembles that of the relationship Christ has with the church and with you. When you do something out of order or out of the will of God, doesn't he correct you? The same process should be able to happen with your spouse. If you do something that is not befitting the image of Christ, your spouse should be able to tell you that or show you that. This is a hard concept to walk as well as explain to others, but if your spouse only has your best interest at heart, then all pruning, forming and shaping, although it may be painful, should feel like they love you.

Agape love, the unusual kind of love will not be formed overnight. It takes a conscious effort at least in the beginning, but it can be done. Using God's love for us as the example helps guide you in the right direction, but being able to do this is predicated on you having a relationship with him. You cannot expect someone to love you like this if they have never experienced it for themselves through their own personal relationship with God. If you or your mate can't even relate to what this chapter is about, then we suggest, you pause here and take some time and spend with God getting to know Him so that he can help guide you and change your heart. This chapter is the longest in the book because it is the center of what we believe can turn a marriage around. We believe that the love of

God and showing that kind of love to your spouse can turn your relationship around or make it so much better. We are a living testimony to this fact and are really sharing this out of our experience as well as the many other couples we have worked with. Before proceeding, take some time in prayer with God and ask him to open your heart to hear the rest of what we share in the book to help make your marriage and your relationship with him better.

Application Questions:

1. How will you walk out your role as servant leader?

2. How will you walk out the role of submission?

3. Is there anything standing in the way of the two of you becoming one, and if so, what do you plan to do about it?

4. How can you show your spouse that you love them unconditionally?

5. What changes need to be made in you so that you can love your spouse as Christ loves the church?

Be willing to:

1. Grow spiritually so that you can love your spouse the way Christ loves us.

2. Serve your spouse from a loving perspective.

3. Lead your spouse from a loving perspective.

4. Show love even when the other is unlovable and create the cycle of love.

5. Remove whatever barriers there are to the two of you becoming one.

Ask God:

To renew your covenant with you and your spouse before you move to the next portions of the book so that your heart will be softened and your ears are ready to hear how to make your relationship the best that it can be.

STAGE THREE

UNDER NEW COVENANT

CHAPTER EIGHT

What Do You Want From Me?

What are your expectations of your spouse? What are your needs? What do you value as important? What happens if your spouse doesn't fulfill those expectations and needs? Are you disappointed, hurt, angry or even resentful ..... maybe all of the above? Can you recall a time that an expectation that you had wasn't met by your spouse? Was that expectation verbalized or did you think that you told them what you expected?

Expectations in marriages are usually based on those things that we value. Sometimes we can clearly see what we value in an expectation that we have, but there are many times that the expectations are ones that come from our history of our families as well as past relationships. When these expectations arise it may take a little digging on your part to see where that comes from.

I'll give you an example, when I was a kid, if I got sick, my mom would pamper me, baby me and you could always expect a bowl of chicken noodle soup, some Town House crackers and a ginger ale. Well when we got married, I expected the same from my husband. It is kind of one of those unwritten rules that when people get sick, you know what to do because that is what "all" people do or I would think that's what you "should" do. Those two words "all" and "should" will get you into a lot of trouble. Well, lo and behold, I would get sick and my husband would do the exact opposite of the whole babying thing. He would act like I had the Ebola virus or something deadly like that and bolt the other way, barely checking on me (or at least that's how I felt) and basically staying away. How do you think I felt? Yeah, I felt, hurt, disappointed, angry and even resentful, especially if he got sick, because I was thinking, you want me to baby you when you get sick, but you won't do the same for me.

Many of you in this situation would do just what I did, think to yourself, the next time he gets sick, I'm going to treat him like he treated me to show him how it feels or the next he gets sick I'm going to baby him to show him exactly what I'm looking for. Why not just tell them, when I get sick I would like for you to …. ? Why, because many of us aren't aware of our expectations until a situation or conversation arises.

Expectations, by far, are the most underrated if not ever talked about subject in a marriage, but it can be the most deadly to a marriage if not dealt with. Expectations are based on values and needs. These are both things that are not necessarily on the surface so they require a little digging. So let's dig.

What are some of the things that you would like your spouse to do that would make you happy? For example, would you like him to take out the trash daily, wash the car, go to work daily, and pray with you? Would you like for your wife to cook on a regular basis, do the laundry, keep up with your children's homework, and have sex with you 3 times a week? How do you find out what your expectations are? Write down some of the things that your spouse has done that makes you happy. Now, write down some of the things that your spouse has not done and how you felt when they were not done. If you wrote anything like hurt, disappointed, angry, or resentful... these are some of your expectations. For example, if you wrote, it would make me happy if my wife would have sex with me 3 times a week and we haven't had sex in over a month, you are probably feeling a little angry or even resentful. If you wrote, it would make me happy if my husband would spend more time helping with the children at least in the evening before bed, but I have to beg him to give a bath, you may be feeling a little hurt, disappointed or angry. These two examples are ones that come up over and over again in marriages, but they are pretty much ones that could be on the surface.

Now, write down some of the things that you value. For example, do you value education, relationship with God, relationship with family, money, time alone, time together, family time, timeliness, cleanliness, physical appearance, fidelity? Values can be lessons we were taught growing up like take care of your brothers and sisters, protect one another, always be respectful, education is important so make good grades, being a Christian is important and you must attend church every Sunday, never allow anyone to come in between your relationship. These are just a few examples, but the things we value are usually the things that we hold dear but we really don't talk about them, they are the unspoken things that govern your life. They are kind of like the playbook to your life. If you value relationship to family, it may be important to you that your wife has a good relationship with your mother and if she doesn't, you may see it as a thorn in your side because you are caught in the middle. If you value money, it may be important to you to make sure that your family has a clear budget and follow that budget to the letter. Going a little deeper some of our values then signal what our deepest needs are.

We all have a need for food, water, shelter some sense of safety and security, stability, and a sense of being loved and accepted. Many of our behaviors are then based on these needs. Did you ever wonder why you felt uneasy if there was less than a certain amount of money in your bank account? Did you ever think about why you fight so hard to get others to like you? Did you ever think about why you would only date people who had some sense of job stability? So, what are some of your needs?

For men the highest need in a relationship is to be respected and for a woman, the highest need in a relationship is for safety and security. This is why most times when speaking to men about issues in their marriage they will say they just want their wife to respect them. Then the same is true for women with their need, often times women's needs are voiced in their concerns for their family and herself and the need for safety and security is played out rather than stated overtly. For example, your wife says I'm worried that the money that the two of you have been making will not be enough to cover your bills this month. This statement could be made out of your wife's need for safety and security. Women want to feel like their home is safe and stable and that her needs and her children's needs are taken care of without the whole world being turned upside down. If you can meet the underlying need of your spouse, you will have hit a major stride in your relationship. As was stated before, some if not most expectations, values and needs go unspoken, but are truly ingrained in you and your spouse.

You can be brave at this point and ask yourself, do you know what your spouse's expectations are? If so, have you been meeting those expectations? On a scale of 1 – 10 overall, with 1 being the lowest and 10 being the highest, have you been meeting your spouse's expectations, values, and needs? What would your spouse say and would they give you the same score? Using the same scale, what number would you rate your spouse on how they have met your expectations, values, and needs? Would they agree? Would you be satisfied with the job performance rating that they gave you? If the way you treat your spouse was rated like a job performance, would you be fired today?

At this point, write down the expectations that you have of your spouse? Then, look for where these expectations come from? Are they based on family history, your own personal relationship history, or both? Of the ones you have written what is the value behind them if any and what need do they fulfill? Now, think about how you would feel if they weren't met. If you said you would be ok if they weren't met, then put those to the side for now and focus on the ones that you wrote, you would feel hurt, disappointed, angry or resentful if they weren't met. The ones that draw the most emotions are the ones that we want you to focus on. These are the ones that we want you to share with your spouse. (Use Figure 8.1 for this exercise) For each one that you have written give a number of importance 1 being the lowest and 10 being the highest. Then we want you to rate how you think your spouse is doing meeting that expectation on a scale of 1-10 and your spouse should do the same.

Expectation/ Value/ Need	Rate the importance of the expectation on scale of 1-10	Rate how your spouse is meeting this expectation on a scale of 1-10	I am willing	I am willing but...	I am not willing

Expectation / Value / Need Graph Figure 8.1

After you have done this, you and your spouse should exchange papers, and for each answer you've written, your spouse should check, I am willing with no questions, I am willing but, or I am not willing. Then you and your spouse should talk about which ones are of the highest importance to both of you, how you would feel if it weren't met and what you need from one another so that the expectation, value, need is met. You should also discuss the ones that you or your spouse have said they are willing to meet but and the ones they have said they are not willing to meet. Make sure you are clear on what your expectations are and even give examples if needed. So, if you say, it would make me happy if you would help with the laundry, what does help look like? Is that just washing and drying? Does that include folding and putting away? How many times a week do you mean? You can't get mad if they don't meet an expectation if you were not clear on what the expectation was in the first place.

There will be times that you have an expectation and your spouse just can't or won't be able to meet it. Is this one a deal breaker for you? How will you handle it? Sometimes talk around expectations can be difficult, but you have to be willing to have the tough conversations. What if one of your expectations is that your spouse have a relationship with your mother and every time she tries your mother rejects her and on this sheet you find out that your wife is now not willing to have that relationship? How are you going to feel about that? What needs to be said in the conversation about this? Why does your wife feel this way? Is there room for a compromise?

Marriage at times is a dance of compromise and just because you want something and you've spelled it out clearly, doesn't mean that you will get it. Let's say an expectation is that

126

there is a home cooked meal 5 times a week. That's pretty clear. Well, your spouse checks the box, I am willing but. Now, there needs to be some conversation around this or negotiation. The compromise could be, we will have a home cooked meal five times a week if the wife cooks 3 and the husband cooks 2 and on the night that you cook, the other one cleans up the kitchen. Expectations can be negotiated and compromised on and you can still feel like the need is being met and the value that you placed on it is still being appreciated.

Where do these expectations come from? Are these expectations from what you saw or didn't see in the home that you grew up in or are they from your past relationships? Our past experiences really do shape how we see the world and how we expect that others will operate in the world. If there is something that you have never seen before, what frame of reference do you have for that? For example, with the state of the divorce rate and the rate of children born to unwed mothers, many of you reading this book grew up in a single parent household. If this is the case, where did you see someone who was married and what did you learn from their marriage? Did you learn what it looked like to be a wife, mother, husband or father? Was it a positive example of these roles or a negative one? What if you've never seen anyone in the role of wife or husband, what reference point do you have? These points can make it difficult to act out these roles in your marriage because you may not have any idea of what your expectations could be other than maybe the ones you've seen on TV.

Some of the expectations we bring into the relationship are from our past or our baggage and some of them should have never made the ride. They are unrealistic, unfair and oftentimes impossible for the other person to meet. These expectations don't fit "your" family (the one that you are creating with your spouse) and they don't fit where you are going. Some of the values that these expectations are based on are flawed and can't go along for the ride. Some examples of flawed values are, you are strong and independent so never lean on a man for anything, not even your husband, never trust a man, all men are dogs, never let your guard down or you will get hurt either emotionally or physically. All men eventually leave, all women want is to spend your money, don't love any woman more than you love your momma, never put your wife ahead of "family", it's okay to have more than one woman as long as you are providing financially at home, women take care of the children and my only role as a man is to provide for the family financially, women can handle it all and I can do whatever I want, I only need a woman so she can cook, clean, have sex with me and take care of my children. You have to do what I want in order to make me happy and if you don't I can leave because it's too hard and you don't make me happy anyway. Have you heard any of these before or seen any of these played out in your or your parent's relationships?

We are all taught lessons in our homes as a child as well as the lessons life teaches us and these lessons begin to shape who we are and what we want. These lessons make up our values, needs and expectations. We bring them with us and they can taint the relationship you have with your spouse if you are not careful. Many women have been taught either by their family members or by their own personal experience to never trust a man. How does this "value" play out in your relationship? How does this affect your relationship? Are you able to fully trust your husband if this is a value for you or is he on a short leash? How can you expect your relationship to flourish if you are always waiting for the other shoe to drop?

Many men have been taught no one should ever come before your mother, not even your wife. Well, that's not biblical. The bible clearly states, many times, that a man should leave his mother and father and cleave to his wife and the two shall become one. How can you expect your wife to want to become one with you when she feels like there is a barrier between the two of you, your mother? This chapter is about you getting to know who you really are so that your spouse can truly speak to the core of who you are based on what you value and need. Everyone has flawed values that go against what God has called for marriage to look like, but only you can change what those values look like so that they line up with the person you want to be and the relationship you want to have. Get rid of those values and expectations that fight against the growth and progression of your relationship.

When there is growth there is also change and expectations can change as well. We know some of you are saying, ah, here we go, as soon as I get this down, here comes something else. You're right, but that's life, people change and grow. Needs change and grow and what you value can also shift. The same expectations you had of your spouse before you had children are not the same once you have children. Some of them you will just let go of naturally and others will have to be renegotiated. Marriage is a lifetime of renegotiations. Some of them will go through an unspoken negotiation and others will have to have the full conversation to be negotiated. You will be able to recognize the ones that need the full negotiation by the feelings that surround them. If you are feeling angry, resentful, hurt, disappointed or even burdened by something, then that issue needs to be discussed and negotiated.

If you used to be the one to do all the laundry with no problem, in fact, truth be told you used to enjoy doing laundry because you had your own system, but now it feels like a burden because you have two children. You are now doing the laundry for four people instead of 2 or even 3. Instead of letting the burden or anger rise up, tell your spouse, I need some help. Lay out what that help looks like. Talk about if your definition of help is something that your spouse can do. Then you have to let them help you with no negative criticism if they don't help in the exact way that you like it done, because then you will make them not want to help.

Being critical about what you expect makes your partner not want to meet that expectation, but being discouraged about an expectation not being met is a totally different story. Sometimes couples get discouraged and have a hard time understanding why their spouse just doesn't get it. You've told them over and over what you need, how you need it, but then they still don't get it. Don't be discouraged. Discouragement is just one foot away from depression if dwelled on too long. No your spouse isn't perfect but neither are you. We know it's hard to deal with some of the disappointments you've faced and they may have even turned into resentment by now. There is always a way back if you're willing to do the work.

It is easy to get discouraged; you asked your husband to do something for you and for whatever reason, he just didn't do it or if he did, it didn't seem like he heard all of what you said. You told your wife that you were looking forward to spending some "alone time" with her later and for the third night in a row she has been tired. You feel rejected and now you are getting discouraged. We told you it's easy to get discouraged.

Discouragement comes out of feelings of rejection no matter how great or small. After a while the rejections begin to mount up and they appear to be more than the times that your husband or wife actually acknowledges and gives you what you've asked for. The mounting rejections are now beginning to increase and cause your discouragement to mount as well. No one wants to feel rejected, especially in their marriage. Rejections can be as simple as you asked your husband to help you look over your resume because you are stepping out on faith to get a new job and he said no you can handle it. Whether his intention was to encourage or discourage, it may feel like rejection. Rejection can also be as big as your spouse has had an affair and now your relationship is crumbling. In some marriages that are struggling they will never have what most people would consider a huge rejection, but they will have a lot of little rejections that continue to pile up on one another until you feel like you are about to explode. You've asked your wife over and over again to keep her side of the room clean, but she does not until one day you just dump all of her things on the floor. You've asked your husband over and over again to help with the laundry because it keeps piling up and overrunning your home, but he does not until one day you stop washing his clothes and lets only his clothes pile up.

How do you get out of these feelings of anger, resentment, tit for tat? What do you do? What do you ask your spouse to do? Do you feel overwhelmed with the discouragement and don't know where to start? Start with you. What is it that you are most discouraged about in your relationship? What is it that if your spouse changed it tomorrow could make you finally feel heard and understood? What is it that you want your spouse to know that if it was done would make you the happiest? The answer to these questions is where you start. Many of these answers will come from the work that you've already done in Figure 8.1. Go back and look at what you said were your expectations and if you felt like those needs were being met. If the ranking you gave them on whether or not your spouse is meeting them is low, then you are probably feeling resentful and possibly feeling rejected because meeting your needs is a way of showing love. So if your spouse is not meeting your needs you may not be feeling loved. Talk to your spouse about your feelings and reassure them that there is no reason for them to get defensive. (People often feel attacked when being asked to change something that they either thought they were doing right or knew they weren't quite up to par but were too proud to admit it.) Only give your spouse one discouragement at a time, then share with them a few (no more than 3) things that if done for you would make you feel much better, understood, and appreciated. If your partner has a hard time understanding your feelings, compare your feelings and what you have been going through with an instance when they felt discouraged, rejected, taken for granted so that they can empathize with what you are going through now.

Marriage is dance that has a delicate balance. Sometimes you get it right and sometimes you miss the mark completely, but you have to be willing to keep trying. Some of the expectations that we've seen come up over and over that cause the most contention and discouragement are division of labor, contrasting views on sexuality and ways of handling money, different energy levels, contrasting views on interacting with in-laws, contrasting desires for participating in recreational activities, contrasting thoughts about family and friends, differences in parenting styles and in religion, contrasting thoughts about what it means to be clean or organized, differences in timeliness and in self- care, contrasting thoughts about roles in the home, differences in attitude towards work(earning money), differences in display of affection.

If you don't remember anything else, remember that you must learn your spouse and continue to learn them on a yearly, monthly and even daily basis. You must know your spouse better that anyone else. Know the desires of their heart and meet them. Don't meet the need that you think they have or the need that most women or men have or the need that your past girlfriend or boyfriend had. Get to know them and their personal needs and meet them. Choose to meet your spouse's needs today even if they don't reciprocate. If for whatever reason your spouse is missing the mark on your expectations and you have discussed it and they still miss the mark and you realize they are not doing this on purpose, this is one of those times that you will need to forgive them for and give them grace. No one is perfect. Getting people to change is hard. Permanent change is even harder. Just know that these changes will not take place overnight and you will have to give them time to permeate. Remember, it's easy to get discouraged, but hopefully these tools that we've shared can help change that and encourage you. Just as we discussed in the last chapter, forgiveness is a cornerstone of your relationship and making it work. Remember love does not keep a record of wrongs and does not keep score, forgive!

Application Questions:

1. How can you meet your spouse's expectations?

2. What if anything do you need to do differently to make sure you are meeting their needs?

3. Are you truly doing all that you can to meet their needs?

4. What expectations and needs do you have that are not being met and how will you talk to your spouse about them?

Be willing to:

1. Dig to see what you expect, value, and need.

2. Have the tough conversations around your expectations, values and needs.

3. Make the necessary corrections in how you respond to your spouse's needs.

4. Be flexible as time passes because expectations and needs change.

Ask God:

To help you meet your spouse's needs. Have the disposition to want to meet those needs. To let go of hurts and resentment . To speak to your spouse about your needs without being angry. To forgive your spouse for past times where they have missed the mark. To love your spouse even when they miss the mark.

How would it feel to have someone not only know your deepest needs, but be willing to fulfill your needs? We all have a need to be loved, heard, understood, and accepted. What if your spouse could be the one to meet those needs? Do you know specifically what your spouse's needs are? Do you know what your needs are for that matter?

CHAPTER NINE

Let Go of the Score

Are there any issues in your relationship that you haven't forgiven your spouse for yet? Are these issues related to rejections that have built up, or has there been a breach of trust? Is there anything from your past or from past relationships that you haven't been able to forgive? Have you been able to forgive yourself for past mistakes? The fact that this chapter is sandwiched between expectations and trust is no accident. We believe that expectations or needs not being met can lead to anger, resentment, feelings of being taken advantage of and hurt feelings. If you have these feelings towards your spouse how can we expect that you would be willing to trust them to take care of you, your feelings and your heart? So, if you have been reading this book, you know we are about to talk about what you can do to bring about change in your relationship and that change begins with you, especially with forgiveness.

"Forgiveness is to set a prisoner free, and to realize the prisoner was you." Corrie Ten Boom

In Matthew 18:21-35 the bible talks about the parable of the unforgiving servant. In this parable, a king forgave his servant of his debts after begging for forgiveness. However, later in the story the servant refused to forgive the debt of one of his fellow servants. Because of this, the servant who was forgiven was turned over to the tormentors. If you keep reading just on to the next chapter, Matthew 19, the bible begins to speak about marriage and divorce. Is it a coincidence that right after the bible speaks of unforgiveness, divorce is discussed?

In marriage you and your spouse will do things that will make the other angry even to the point sometimes that you feel like you are literally seeing red. There will be times that your spouse would have done or said something that you felt was so wrong that you want to seek revenge. However, those are exactly the times when you need to forgive. Lack of forgiveness can feel like a prison sentence like you're being tormented, being held captive by your thoughts.

Marriage is not a tit for tat relationship; you hurt me so now I need to hurt you. Marriage is a relationship full of grace and forgiveness. After all, our relationship models the relationship that Christ has with the church. What if our sins against our spouses, friends, families, strangers and even ourselves were not forgiven? What if God held grudges for as long as we do? You can't hold a grudge and expect that you and your relationship won't be harmed. You can't keep score.

Being unforgiving leads to feelings of anger, resentment, and sometimes depression and anxiety; it is important to forgive. Forgiveness ultimately is not about the other person and more about you. Forgiveness is a release for you and your jail sentence. Unforgiveness is a prison sentence for the one who has been wronged. You have to forgive in order to be free. We know that this is easier said than done and it is a constant choice that has to be made, but it is a choice nonetheless that needs to be made. If you choose forgiveness, then prayer and faith are a part of the equation, because out of our own strength and will, we would exact revenge for the hurts others have caused us. Which will you choose, to forgive or to hold a grudge; freedom or a prison sentence?

1. Name the actions here that your partner has done to you that you have yet to forgive them for?

_____

_____

_____

_____

_____

_____

_____

_____

2. Name the actions that your partner has done that you have forgiven them for?

_____

_____

_____

_____

_____

_____

_____

_____

3. What's the difference between the two lists? Why have you forgiven some and not the others?

_____

_____

_____

_____

_____

_____

_____

_____

_____

When people think about unforgiveness, they usually think about the big things such as infidelity, publicly doing something that hurts or is embarrassing. What about those smaller things? What about the times that you've asked for something and you weren't given it? What if you have an expectation that you've shared and you think it's very important and for whatever reason your partner has not followed through with it? What about the number of times you have approached your spouse for sex and they've turned you down? Any time there is a possibility for resentment, for a word spoken or deed done, there is an opportunity that you may have to forgive your spouse. So, if you think about it that way, how many times in a day do you forgive your spouse?

We forgive our spouses daily for acts they display or words they speak, we are just not aware that's what we're doing. We're giving them the benefit of the doubt. The problem comes in when we place more value on the action than we do on our spouse or the love that we have for them. We'll give you an example.

You have asked your spouse to please help more around the house. You shared with them that this really means a lot to you. Acts of service is your love language. You shared that you really appreciate the help because at the end of the night it gives you more time to spend with one another. The first few times, your spouse helped out. After about a month they fell off, again. You seem to keep having the same conversation, but they just don't get it. So now, you're becoming increasingly frustrated and are beginning to resent the fact that while you are cleaning, your spouse is watching TV, on the phone, on the computer, anything else but helping you. You begin to think that they are doing this on purpose. Do remember in chapter 3 we talked about the ABC's of change. Act -> Belief -> Choice. The act is your spouse is not helping out, the belief is they are doing this on purpose, the choice is you becoming angry and now acting on that anger. Right there in the "Belief" is where the change will come. This is where you activate giving your partner, the benefit of the doubt and replace the negative feelings with grace, mercy and a willingness to look past their faults. So now your choice is to forgive instead of wallowing in being hurt, angry, resentful etc., because these feelings can have you spiral downward emotionally.

What does spiraling downward into anger, hurt, resentment, depression, anxiety look like? Let's look at the same scenario we laid out above. You've asked your spouse for help, they help for about a month, then they fall off. You notice them doing everything but helping. Instead of bringing it to their attention, you let it linger and fester and you begin to say to yourself, he didn't want to help me anyway. He was just helping so that I would get off his back because he complains that I nag. He really wanted to be doing something else and now his true colors are really showing. I wish he would have told me from the beginning that he really didn't want to help. He got my hopes up and now he has let me down once again, as usual. I can't count on him for anything. I'll just do it myself. My mother always said if you want something done right, you gotta do it yourself. Remind me, why am I with him if I have to do everything myself. Does this sound vaguely familiar? Have there been times that you have been guilty of this? What would happen if you just gave them the benefit of the doubt and forgave them for falling off and then just told them that you still need their help?

Forgiveness looks like being able to recognize the truth about the situation, not the spiral of emotions that can taint reality. Did my spouse say or do whatever it was intentionally to hurt me or did they do it because they were unaware of its impact? Understanding the difference could help salvage a lot of situations that we may have let run in a different direction in our heads.

Forgiveness is one of the cornerstones of Agape Love because without it, there is no way that you can love the way Christ loved and there is no way that you can become one with your spouse. How can you become one if in between the two of you is the argument that you had last week about who does their share of the housework? If we let our every day issues get in the way of our relationship, we are creating an atmosphere of division and one that is counterproductive to becoming one.

One of our favorite things about this type of love is that it doesn't keep score. What does that mean? It means, when your husband does something that really gets on your nerves, you don't keep an account of how many times he has done this and then use it as ammunition the next time the two of you have an argument. Not keeping score means, when your wife says that she's tired and wants to go to sleep, you don't say to her, this is the 15th time this year that you have told me no and if you don't get it together, Michelle at work will. Keeping score means that you are more focused on the problem rather than the solution and that you are more focused on the negative rather than how to fix it.

Even if your spouse has done something that you feel like they should know better by now, because you have told them one million times and they keep doing it, because they know it bothers you and as you're reading this, you're thinking of that thing and getting angrier and angrier. Come back, take a deep breath and give them the benefit of the doubt that they are not doing that thing on purpose and even if they are, you are going to move forward and not keep score. You are going to start and keep the Cycle of Love going. You are able to do this because you have forgiven them. There is no way that you could move through the cycle and keep score, if you have not forgiven them. Forgiveness is key in this relationship because your spouse is usually one of, if not, the closest person to you, so they know what buttons to push. Sometimes they push buttons even when they are not aware because you care for them that much that whatever they do means a lot to you whether what they do is good or bad.

How do you forgive? What about those major issues that have happened in your relationship that have made it harder and harder to forgive? What if there was a betrayal of your trust?

143

Forgiveness, first starts with a willingness to forgive. You can't look at it as an obligation, but more of something you want to do. Forgiveness comes from compassion and grace. Throughout the bible, there are examples of forgiveness, a few examples are when Joseph forgave his brothers for all of their cruelty towards him, Hosea forgave his wife Gomer for all of her infidelity and Jesus forgave those who persecuted him.

We are called to forgive as a part of who we are as Christians, but when done only out of our Christian duty, forgiveness is not real. You have to want to release those who have wronged you and be willing to let those negative feelings go that may be associated with what they have done to you. **Ephesians 4:31-32 (Amplified Bible)** [31]Let all bitterness and indignation and wrath (passion, rage, bad temper) and resentment (anger, animosity) and quarreling (brawling, clamor, contention) and slander (evil-speaking, abusive or blasphemous language) be banished from you, with all malice (spite, ill will, or baseness of any kind). [32]And become useful and helpful and kind to one another, tenderhearted (compassionate, understanding, loving-hearted), forgiving one another (readily and freely), as God in Christ forgave you.

Being able to forgive allows you the freedom in your relationship to move forward and not be bound by past hurts that have piled up. Forgiveness is a selfless act initially as a gift to the other person but ultimately becomes a gift for you because you get to release your anger, resentment, frustration and irritation. Forgiveness starts with a decision that you will not let this thing be more important than your relationship. Then deciding if this is something that you can simply let go of because you have given your spouse the benefit of the doubt and you realize that whatever was said or done was not intentional or deciding that it should be addressed because this is something that could possibly be detrimental to your relationship in the long run. If you are deciding to let it go, then do that, don't continue to bring it up reminding the person of what they have done to wrong you. (Don't keep score.)If you are doing this, you have not truly let it go

If you have decided that this is one of those times that the issue needs to be discussed before you can forgive, we suggest you follow The Rules of Engagement that we have laid out for you in Chapter 11 on how to communicate and deal with conflict. Once you have discussed whatever the issue is and have come to some sort of resolution, now is the time for forgiveness because the final resolution should bring about some sense of peace.   Often times, people continue to hold on to something because they don't have peace about the resolution or once the resolution was reached everyone didn't stick to what each person said they would do. The peace that is felt moves you towards forgiveness because you want to continue the feeling and not be drawn back into the issue. The problem with this is once you feel this peace, you may try to avoid discussing issues because you feel if you avoid the issues, you can keep the peace. This is a VERY wrong move, without discussion and resolution resentment builds, which is the antithesis of peace.

The resolution, however doesn't always include their repentance or saying sorry. We know some of you are saying, "why even discuss it if my wife or my husband isn't going to apologize". Those feelings are completely understandable, but remember what we said, forgiveness is more about you than it is them. Forgiveness is to set you free from the prison of unforgiveness, spiraling thoughts, and negative beliefs. Your spouse does not have to apologize before you forgive them. Just like forgiveness is really an issue between you and God, so is the issue of their repentance. Only God can truly convict your partner so that they feel compelled to apologize or turn away from the words or actions you want them to apologize for. Release even your desire to see them repentant. If you are in prayer for the restoration of your relationship, a part of that is God working behind the scenes to allow your partner to be repentant and work on their end to make amends. Using the filter of God's grace, love and compassion for you and your faults, will help you find the same compassion when you need to forgive your spouse. When your spouse does or says something so outrageous or they just keep doing that thing they know you don't like, use God's compassion as a filter. See their issue, transgression, sin through the eyes of God, through his love for them, through his love for you.

Forgiveness is also linked to faith. We must believe that God cares for our every need and if we pray for restoration, that he will do whatever it takes to make that happen. Forgiveness is also about trust in God that he can give you the strength needed to show the type of unconditional, agape love that he has called you as a husband or a wife to have towards your spouse. We are equipped to handle the assignment of marriage if we trust God to give us the tools we need.

There are times, however, you must seek support or wise counsel to help you move through the issues that could be causing a barrier to you forgiving your spouse. Support comes in many different forms, from talking with a friend, an accountability partner, your minister, or seeking counseling, whichever you choose, but there needs to be a clear understanding that the support you seek is not only for you but for your relationship. If the person is not able to help you and your relationship, then they are not the right person for you to go to for support. And as always, seek God's counsel through prayer. The time that it takes to process the issues that you are having with your spouse varies from one person to the next. For some with issues that may not be as severe, it could be days, but for others whose issue is much more corrosive it could take months to process how you feel. Once you've sought the support you need and you are able to address the issue or issues that are plaguing your relationship, a sense of satisfaction and a sense of peace can be felt and you can then make the choice to forgive.

Forgiveness is a behavior that can be learned, the more you put it into practice the easier it becomes. Forgiveness is drawn from a well of love and positive feelings, which is why you went through the steps of acceptance and understanding in chapter 4, appreciation in chapter 5, friendship in chapter 6 and love in chapter 7. It is much easier to forgive someone you love, are friends with, feel like they accept and appreciate you, and are not out to take you for granted. All of these previous chapters and steps make the ability to forgive your spouse a lot easier. You want to forgive them because you have created a well of good will, a well of generosity and of giving.

The good thing about forgiving your spouse is that it releases you from the burden of carrying frustration, anger or resentment. It also releases your spouse and shows them that you really are sincere in your walk when you say you love them unconditionally. Unforgiveness puts limits on your love for your spouse. The way that you truly know that you have forgiven them is when you are able to talk about whatever the offense was and you no longer have the feelings of hurt, frustration, anger or resentment surrounding the issue.

The inability to forgive in a marriage can be the cancer that is killing your relationship and the cause of why you may want to divorce. Your husband or wife is not perfect. They will do something else that you don't like. They will do something else to hurt you. (Hopefully not on purpose.) You have to decide if being angry, resentful or even seeking revenge is the marriage you want to have.

We truly believe that the bible is the true source that you can use as a guide for your life and the bible speaks of the feelings that are associated with unforgiveness; bitterness, wrath, anger, clamor, evil and malice. How many of you have felt this way after your spouse has done or said something you didn't like, and if it wasn't resolved quickly, how long did it take for the situation to be rectified? Holding grudges, keeping score, returning evil for evil destroys marriages, period.

Forgiveness in a marriage is one of the greatest acts of love you can give your mate. Write down what you forgive your partner for here and then tell them. They may not even be aware that you had been holding on to some of these things.

_____

_____

_____

_____

_____

_____

_____

Application Questions:

1. What can you do today to forgive your spouse?

2. How can you show your spouse that they are forgiven?

3. How can you show your spouse that you are at peace with the issues and that you want to move forward? What can you say?

4. What will you do when you feel like they are reverting back to a behavior you feel you have already forgiven them for?

5. What role does your relationship with God, your faith and your trust in God play in your ability to forgive?

Be willing to:

1. Recognize the Issues that are causing the hurt, anger, frustration or bitterness. Recognize what has you keeping score.
2. Pray and ask God to help you forgive the cause of your frustration or anger.
3. Pray and ask God for restoration of your relationship.
4. Resolve within yourself that you will not hold on to the negative feelings or the behavior that made you hurt, frustrated, or angry.
5. Release your spouse and yourself from the prison of whatever it is that they have done or said that needs to be forgiven.
6. Speak to them about what has been done, but you are not responsible for making them apologize or make

amends. (The forgiving process is for you to be released)

7. Create a plan to help you forgive them, when you recognize the same behavior that is coming up again.
8. Seek support on those issues that you are having difficulty forgiving.
9. Appreciate the peace, and the sense of unloaded burden when you have truly forgiven.
10. Remember the grace and compassion that God has given you when he forgave you for your sins and still is forgiving you daily.

Ask God:

To help you forgive your spouse for their past, present and future transgressions. To help you forgive yourself, your past, the people who have hurt you. To help you see these moments as a way to strengthen your marriage and your relationship with Him rather than something that will tear your marriage apart. To help you not keep score.

CHAPTER TEN

In God We Trust

Do you trust your wife? Do you trust your husband? Do you feel safe with them? Ask yourself the following questions to see how much you trust your spouse. Can you trust your spouse with all of you? Can you trust your spouse not to hurt you? Can you trust your spouse to respect you? Can you trust your spouse to not repeat the issues of your past? Can you trust your spouse with your needs?

Trust is a fragile thing and it needs love, attention and care. Trust means that no matter what comes up in our relationship, you will still love me. Can you lay out all of your past issues and baggage, all the skeletons in your closet and trust that your spouse will still love you? Trust means being honest with not only your spouse but also with yourself. Trust means that I can rely on you and have confidence in the fact that you will do what you said you would do and what you've said is based on the truth.

Trust is a Foundation to Your Relationship

Relationships are based on trust. Your marriage is based on trust. The ability to trust your spouse provides the stability and dependability that any marriage needs to be able to withstand the storms that are guaranteed to come your way. Marriage is like building a house. All homes are built on a foundation, just like your marriage. If there is a crack in the foundation, major damage can be done to the home if it is not repaired. Creating an atmosphere of trust in your relationship comes from being consistent in word and deed as well as being open and honest.

Trust is a muscle that gets a workout in relationships. I have to trust that you are where you say you are; trust that you are going to do what you say you will do; trust that you will be faithful; trust that you will honor me when in the presence of others; that you will take care of my emotions; will respect me; will be honest with me; have my back in good and bad times. Trust is the backbone of your relationship. Trust is if I get in a car accident, I know you will take care of me. Trust is if we have a child with an illness we can work it out together. Trust is that if I lose my job, you won't lose respect for me.

Being able to trust your mate means there are no secrets between you and that no one could say anything to you about your spouse, where they have been, who they have been with or what they have been doing, because you literally know your spouse like the back of your hand. You know your mate so well that if someone said, Mike has been going to Lucky's bar every day after work and been talking to this women, there would be no need for you to flinch because either they were mistaken about seeing Mike there because he was home every day at that time, or you knew he was there and who he was with and you were well aware of the conversations because Mike came home every day and told you about it. The problem here comes in when Mike has decided to leave out that he has been going to the bar every day because he knows how you feel about him hanging out after work, so he decided to tell a little white lie figuring you would never find out. Those little white lies will get you in a lot of trouble, every time.

We've had couples who have gotten into some of their worst arguments around the issue of being completely open with their spouses about everything and having the mindset that I have nothing to hide. This has been a particular issue for newly married men who have been used to being single and not having to be accountable to anyone else since they left their parent's home. In fact, some of them have bristled so hard because they feel like they are back home with their mommas instead of their wives. Men see this as their wives checking up on them to make sure they aren't doing anything they're not supposed to be doing. On the other hand, most women see it as, I just want to know what's going on because I feel better, feel safer and secure when I know where you are and who you are with. Now of course there are people on both ends of the spectrum where they don't want to discuss where they are because they truly do have something they are trying to hide and the other end where they are checking up on you because they really don't trust you and need to know where you are at all times.

How Women Interpret Trust

Nothing erodes trust faster than saying one thing and then doing another. This is a point that many women have issue with. Many women have been misled in this area in so many ways that it can be hard for them to trust you and let their guard down. Have you ever wondered why your wife seems to be fighting you all the time on decisions that really don't seem to be that big of a deal? Trust, someone has let her down in the past and that someone may even be you so it is hard for her to trust that you will do what you said you would do. Now some of you are saying that I have never given her a reason not to trust me, yet she doesn't trust me. What should I do? Be consistent, women need to see that you are consistent in your talk as well as your walk. She needs to see that you truly mean what you say and even though the way you handled a certain situation does remind her of how her dad, mom, or ex handled the situation, with consistency she will see that you are not them and that she can trust you.

How Men Interpret Trust

Ladies, men have issues with trust when they feel disrespected. That means they won't trust you if you go through their things, check their phones, emails, go through their twitter, facebook or any other social media account, if they have never given you a reason not to trust them. This is where men put their guard up and it can look like they are trying to keep secrets. No man wants to feel like his woman is trying to be his mother or some other authority figure in his life and this is a sure fire way for him not to trust that you have his best interest at heart.

Barriers to Trust

The inability to trust your mate feels like they aren't dependable. It feels like the areas you should lean on them for you have to lean on others. The inability to trust your spouse makes it hard for you to lean on them in stressful situations, because they were not there for you one way or the other.

Some barriers to trust are:

Lack of transparency – This is simply not telling your spouse the whole truth about a situation to avoid them becoming upset or you trying to protect them from something that you feel would upset them.

Dishonesty – This is just out and out lying to your spouse about whatever the issue may be.

A history of being deceived or hurt in the past by your spouse or others – This is bringing past issues into your relationship where others have hurt you through their lies so now it is hard for you to trust your present partner.

A history of abuse, physical, emotional, or sexual – This issue is one that has come up with some of the couples we have worked with and often times both people are unaware of how deeply these wounds can affect their relationship. Abuse in and of itself is a betrayal of trust and it usually shatters the abused person's ability to trust others again for fear of being hurt. The reactions to this are different, some people are overly clingy in that they will do whatever you want to please you so that you don't hurt them like their abuser did; some people will have their guard up so that you can't get close to them; then others are more aggressive in that they will hurt you before you get a chance to hurt them.

None of these scenarios work well in a relationship where trust, transparency and intimacy are the goals. If this is a situation you find yourself in, it is important that you seek professional help to deal with the issues of your past and how they are affecting your present.

Projection means placing your feelings on a situation that may not necessarily be the truth. There have been many times we've had men and women omit a portion of their story to their spouse either because they are trying to in their minds protect them or they are trying to hide something they feel that their spouse will react to negatively. When your spouse reacts to something in a way that feels negative, it's almost like when you were a kid and you would get in trouble. Once you learned what that something was, you did your best to avoid it, even if that meant not divulging the whole truth about something so you could avoid getting into trouble. Have you taken that behavior into your marriage? Have you ever not told your husband or wife something because you were "avoiding getting into trouble"?

Ok fellas, have you ever told your wife that you were coming home straight from work, but instead you stopped off to see a friend, but when she asked what took so long you gave her this long convoluted story about how you ended up leaving later than you thought then there was traffic and oh you had to make a quick stop at the store, and blah, blah, blah. You did all of this to avoid your wife becoming angry because you think she doesn't like this friend or the fact that you were hanging out with a friend while she was at home with the children. Ultimately, when we ask women what upsets them in these scenarios it's not that the husband went to spend time with his friend, it's the fact that he felt the need to hide it from her in this web of lies. The wife then begins to think, what else is he lying about?

Ladies, have you ever told your husband you were just going to run into the mall to pick up one item and you end up going over the amount you were set to spend because you saw this pair of shoes, "you had to have"? Instead of telling your husband you just overspent, you hide the shoes in the trunk of the car because he will never go in there. You do this to avoid being scolded by your husband because that's how it feels whenever you have one of these conversations about your shopping and spending. When asked most husbands issue is that the wife feels the need to hide the shoes from him and not tell him what was spent because ultimately the amount spent affects the household budget.

Reliving how you tried to avoid getting into trouble as a kid in your marriage causes many problems for couples. Instead of living in this moment with your spouse, you are projecting onto them what your parents did or a previous boyfriend or girlfriend did. Is that fair to your spouse? This area can be sticky in that you decide after reading this to change how you act in these situations and instead of telling only a portion of the story, you are transparent and share the whole story and your spouse reacts negatively to the whole truth. What do you do with that? Do you revert back to what you used to do? Do you say to them that's why I don't tell you anything because I knew how you would react? Do you tell them I am working on making sure I am transparent about everything and I need you to work on how you react because I want to be able to talk with you without feeling like I need to hide things because of the way you are going to react? Being able to talk to your spouse openly about everything is a freeing feeling, but you have to have a spouse who is willing and able to handle the complete truth.

Lack of Faith in Spouse

Faith is a huge part of the ability to trust your mate; not only faith in them, but faith in God. A wise woman once said, "trust is a battle between the Holy Spirit and your emotions". Sometimes we can allow our feelings and what has been done to overshadow what God says about your marriage and relationship. God never promised that the relationship would be easy. Too often people leave God out of the equation of their relationship and their everyday issues. God is not just concerned with the big issues in your life, but He's concerned with the small ones as well.

The ability to trust in your relationship relies on a track record, a history of what has been done or for some what has not been done. Trust is knowing that you pray for me even when I'm not around. Trust builds relationships and can also tear them down when it is broken, which can lead to a lack of faith in your spouse; a lack of faith that you will meet my needs based on your track record, a lack of faith that you're being honest with me, a lack of faith that you are trustworthy. Lack of faith can lead to the breakdown of trust in your relationship with your spouse. But who is it that you don't trust? Is it your spouse or God or both?

What Does God Have to do with Trust

Trust is not just between you and your spouse, it is also between you and God. You must trust that God has a hand in this relationship and your future and that he knows what he is doing. We talked earlier about submission in the context of love, it is also an act of not only trusting your spouse, but God as well. When you are submitting to your spouse, you are trusting that they are talking to God to find out what is best for your family and is acting in a way that benefits the whole family and not them as an individual and if they're not, you have to trust God that he will convict them and make it right. (To be transparent, there are times when I have moments of not trusting my husband because of past mistakes that he has made and poor decisions, but those are also the moments when I have to talk to myself and God and remind myself of who my husband is now, not who he used to be.)

Carrying and bringing up past issues and mistakes is a prime example of something that can erode the trust In a relationship. You have to allow your spouse the opportunity and room to grow and change. If in the midst of the change, you continually remind your spouse of what they used to do and don't recognize what they are doing, they will not trust you not to hurt them. When people are hurt they do one of two things, they hurt back or they retreat. Don't create a vicious cycle in your relationship of tit for tat because you can't let some things go and forgive. Oh there is that word again, forgive, without this word, many marriages wouldn't survive. Forgive your spouse for past mistakes and let them go especially if it is an area that they are actively working on. Forgiving your spouse will help you trust your spouse.

What do You do When Trust Has Been Broken

How can you regain trust once it is lost? How can you ever trust him again after he …? How can you trust her again after she …? You can regain your trust through restoration. Restoration is bringing the relationship back to the place it once was before the loss of trust. How do you do that? You take small steps. You talk about all of the things we have discussed in the book thus far by using the tools that we lay out in Chapter

10. You talk about what has happened in your relationship to get you to this point and where you believe it went wrong. Ask yourself all of the questions in each chapter and have your spouse do the same. Be a detective to figure out the precise moment when you truly said, I don't trust my spouse anymore. What was that moment? For some people, it is an out and out specific behavior that you can easily pinpoint, like infidelity, for others it is more of a latent issue like wanting your husband to be a leader in your home and pray with you or your wife has disrespected you more than once in front of others by talking about how she doesn't like the way you handle certain things in your relationship. If I want you to lead me through prayer and it is not being done, I don't know if I trust that you are doing it on your own when I'm not around? If I can't trust that you will have my back while I'm standing in front of you, how can I trust that you won't throw me under the bus to our children? All of these are valid statements. Do any of these ring true for you? If they don't, are there any that you can think of that might? We talk about you taking responsibility for your role in the issues in your home. (We will discuss this in more depth in chapter 10) What role have you played in the eroding of the trust in your relationship? What role do you want to play in the restoration of that trust?

The ability to restore your relationship calls for:

1. Being transparent and completely honest with your spouse at all times; even in those moments when you feel like they can't handle the honesty.
2. Being consistent with what you say and do. Making sure that you follow through with what you've said you would do, and if you can't, being honest about it to your mate. For example, you and your spouse have discussed

expectations and your husband has said he wants you to support his new business venture and you have promised that you would, however after a few months of things being a little rocky you're not so sure about the business. Instead of shielding him like you did in the past from your true emotions about the business, be transparent and share your concerns and give him the opportunity to address your concerns.

3. Making sure that there are appropriate boundaries in place if there are people, places, or things that have eroded your trust. An example would be if you have had an affair with someone, that person and all of their information is deleted from all of your contact information. You no longer have any conversation with them even if it is work related. You no longer put yourself in situations that would tempt you to step back into the affair with that person or anyone else.

4. Showing your spouse that you are committed to your relationship with them and that the issues that have caused a breach in your trust are no longer there.

5. Time, the ability to trust again takes time. You will not trust your spouse completely again over night. Allow time for whatever wounds that may have been caused to heal. Seek help if necessary. Create accountability partners who want to see your marriage succeed, but give it time.

6. Praying for the restoration of your marriage, even if the marriage you had before wasn't what you want now. You are praying for the restoration of your marriage to the place that God wants for your marriage.

How Lack of Trust Can Affect Intimacy

You must trust that whenever your spouse is not with you they are being true to you no matter who is in their presence. You have to trust and have faith that even if you are nowhere to be found they are honoring you. We have had so many couples come in with the issue of the husband receiving text messages from friends, old girlfriends, old side pieces, facebook messages, emails, carrier pigeon (no not really the carrier pigeon, just wanted to see if you were paying attention). The messages are almost always sexually explicit and the husband almost always gets caught.

Before he was married, this wasn't a big deal to him or his friends, but now that he is married, this behavior is not appropriate. If you saw a message on your wife's phone of a completely naked man who just happens to be the guy she dated before you, would you be okay with that? If you are not okay with that, then it is not ok to receive sexually explicit messages of any kind from anyone because they take away from your wife's ability to trust that you are not acting on the messages that are being sent. Fellas, trust me this is more of a headache than it is worth. If this picture, email, message etc. isn't worth your marriage, let it go. Trust me your boys will get over it and so will your ex girl.

When the trust is broken at whatever level, the intimacy between you and your spouse is broken and this will affect the closeness you have with your spouse. It will feel like there is a wedge between you. You will feel like it's hard to get close to your spouse and they may even feel distant. The lack of intimacy because of the breakdown of trust can then lead to a breakdown in the friendship which will definitely affect your sexual relationship.

The lack of faith in this area could come from your track record of not meeting needs, from her being hurt in the past, or it may have nothing to do with you at all. It could stem from a past relationship or even being let down over time by family. If you don't get to the root of this problem that is affecting the trust in your relationship, it will keep coming up until you address it. Ultimately, the two of you need to have a conversation about what is affecting the trust in your relationship and get to the root of the problem so that you can discover if your actions or the actions of someone else is affecting the intimacy with your spouse.

There are many ways trust can be broken, but as we mentioned, following our plan of restoration can help you reestablish trust and help regain intimacy.

How Trust, Vulnerability and Intimacy Work Together

Trust creates the atmosphere for intimacy and the ability to be vulnerable. Without trust, your spouse won't feel safe enough to let you in on those places that you feel you have a right to be privy to. Being vulnerable with your spouse means that you can share anything with them about you, your past and any skeletons you may have in your closet that you wouldn't share with most people. Being vulnerable means that you trust your spouse enough with your heart not to hurt you or use what you've shared with them to hurt you. Being able to be vulnerable with your spouse is very liberating and freeing.

Imagine that you just found out that your mother is dying of cancer. How would you feel if you couldn't share this with your spouse? Now imagine that you could share this and any other painful or joyous experience with them without the fear of being let down or hurt in any way. Having a spouse that loves and appreciates you, speaks in love to you, accepts you for who you are, works to meet your needs, treats you like a friend, gives you the benefit of the doubt, and forgives you, creates a safe place for you to fall. Now imagine if this really was the description of your relationship at least most of the time, you could be vulnerable, you would feel a sense of intimacy and you would trust your spouse. Establish this type of relationship with your spouse, if you haven't already. This will help you maintain the trust in your relationship.

Application Questions:

1. What has happened if anything to impact the trust in your relationship?
2. Do you trust God to navigate the right path for your relationship?
3. Has the intimacy in your relationship been affected by a lack of trust?
4. Can you feel vulnerable with your spouse? Why or Why not?
5. What can you do to reestablish trust, intimacy and vulnerability?
6. Has something or someone other than your spouse impacted the way you trust your spouse? If so, how do you plan to resolve this?
7. What can you do today to move one step closer to the relationship where you can be completely vulnerable with your spouse?

Be Willing to:

1. Let your guard down.
2. Do whatever it takes to reestablish trust if it has been broken.
3. Let go of whomever or whatever that is standing in the way of complete trust in your relationship.
4. Let God into your relationship and the everyday concerns of your relationship.
5. Be completely honest with your spouse and get rid of the "little white lies"
6. Be vulnerable.
7. Be the safe place for your spouse.

Ask God:

To give you the ability to be completely honest and transparent with your spouse. To trust him implicitly with your relationship. To soften your heart to forgive your spouse if needed and restore your relationship to where he wants it to be. To establish a sense of intimacy and vulnerability in your relationship so that you and your spouse can be closer.

CHAPTER ELEVEN

Speak Life and Not Death

When you are in conflict with your spouse, how do you view it? Do you see conflict as a healthy part of every marital relationship that needs to happen in order for your relationship to grow, or do you see it as a battle that you must win in order to get what you want? Your answer to this may answer your question of why is it every time you and your spouse are in conflict, it becomes a heated battle that no one really wins.

Every marriage will have conflict, it is just a matter of how you deal with the conflict that will determine (1) how much conflict you will have or (2) the outcome of that conflict. When engaging in discussion on issues with your spouse, you can view it from one of two angles, which is either positive or a negative. The positive definition of engagement according to Webster's Dictionary is a promise or pledge, to bind yourself to marry, to attract and hold attention. The negative definition is to enter into conflict with the enemy. Which one has been the definition of your conflict with your spouse? Often times when you are in conflict with your spouse you forget that you are in a union that you pledged to stand together with your spouse and not stand apart as if the two of you are at war. **Mark 3:25** *25 If a house is divided against itself, that house will not be able to stand.*

Even though you have conflict and you may feel that nothing is being accomplished, there is a way to have your engagement in discussion be from a positive standpoint and not the negative. You can deal with conflict from a loving standpoint rather than an adversarial one. You can come from a position of giving agape love, which is defined as a self-giving love, gift love, the love that goes on loving even when the other becomes unlovable. Agape love is the kind of love that Christ gave to us. His love was sacrificial and unconditional and we are to pattern our love for one another after the love that Christ has for us. According to 1 **Corinthians 13: 4-8** love suffers long and is kind, love does not parade itself, is not puffed up, does not behave rudely, does not seek its own, is not provoked, thinks no evil, does not rejoice in iniquity, but rejoices in the truth, bears all things, believes all things, hopes all things and endures all things. From this kind of love we can take clues on how to handle conflict with our spouse even in the midst of anger. The model that we created will help you remember the bottom line when dealing with conflict which is to deal with the conflict from a spirit of AGAPE LOVE. The acronym AGAPE LOVE stands for:

> A – Always create a safe place to talk (by setting ground rules ahead of time)
> G – Gather your thoughts and feelings
> A – Accept responsibility for your role in the conflict
> P – Produce effective communication
> E – Eliminate negative talk (speak the truth in love)

L – Listen carefully and repeat
O – Openly discuss the problem involved in conflict (one at a time)
V- Vow to resolve the issue and follow up (at least one week for smaller issues or an agreed upon time for larger issues)
E – Experience the power of the Holy Spirit through prayer

A – Always Create a Safe Place to Talk (by setting ground rules ahead of time)
Some examples of ground rules are no cursing at each other, no bringing up hurtful things from the past, not allowing others into the conflict unless it is an impartial third party, we will talk on Sundays after church which will be our set time every week. What are some ground rules that you have set up for your communication with your spouse?

_____
_____
_____
_____
_____
_____
_____
_____
_____
_____
_____
_____

Both of you need to feel that you can communicate without, feeling like your words will come back to haunt you. You should be able to be free to communicate openly without fear of reprisal from your spouse or anyone that they may have confided in.

Bible verse: Proverbs 18:21 *Death and life are in the power of the tongue, And those who love it will eat its fruit.*

G – Gather Your Thoughts and Feelings

Sometimes we don't take the time to gather our thoughts and feelings and it can be disastrous. We need to speak with love in our hearts and on our tongue. Has there ever been a time that you said something in the heat of the moment that you wish you could take back, but it was too late, the damage was already done? This point is telling you to take time before you speak. We know that you will become passionate and heated about some issues, but the words you speak can have an impact far beyond your present conversation. All of the verses below point to how speaking in anger either makes you look foolish or creates more anger by pushing your spouse's buttons.

Bible Verses: Proverbs 14:29 *He who is slow to wrath has great understanding, But he who is impulsive exalts folly.*
Proverbs 15:1 *A soft answer turns away wrath, but a harsh word stirs up anger.*
Proverbs 15:28 *The heart of the righteous studies how to answer, But the mouth of the wicked pours forth evil.*
Proverbs 19:11 *The discretion of a man makes him slow to anger, and his glory is to overlook a transgression.*
Proverbs 21:23 *Whoever guards his mouth and tongue keeps his soul from troubles.*

A – ACCEPT RESPONSIBILITY for YOUR Role in the Conflict

Often times we want to place blame on the other person and not take responsibility, but we must take responsibility for our actions. When you accept responsibility you are committed to coming to a conclusion that is best for your marriage, you look to resolve issues through problem solving and when things go wrong, you are willing to own up to your role and essentially bear the burden of the decisions that you have made. This is a hard one for a lot of people. It is much easier to place the blame on others, but the source of your ongoing conflict may stem from your inability to accept your responsibility for your role in the issue and own up to it.

Avoidance is not a strong suit in a relationship, so put on your big girl or big boy pants and "man up". Be willing to apologize and make amends for what you have done wrong. This can be tricky because you have to know the way your spouse apologizes. For some, they just can't outright say I'm sorry or I apologize, and others will gesture in some way that they are sorry. Are you going to hold it against them or hold a grudge if they don't overtly say I'm sorry? Is the gesture that they would do enough for you? If not you need to find out what is and make sure you acknowledge their apology in the form it is given. **Bible Verse: Galatians 5:1-5** *Brethren, if a man is overtaken in any trespass, you who are spiritual restore such a one in a spirit of gentleness, considering yourself lest you also be tempted. 2 Bear one another's burdens, and so fulfill the law of Christ. 3 For if anyone thinks himself to be something, when he is nothing, he deceives himself. 4 But let each one examine his own work, and then he will have rejoicing in himself alone, and not in another. 5 For each one shall bear his own load.*

P – Produce Effective Communication

Communicate at an agreed upon time that is good for both of you. For example, not after 9pm, because one of you will get too sleepy, or only after the kids are in bed. This does not mean that you consistently say that this is not a good time so that you can avoid the conversation. If you say that this is not a good time you must come back with a time that is good for you. Talk to each other without distractions, such as the TV, cell phones, video games, computers or children in order to give your undivided attention to what is being said. If someone does call during your conversation, don't pick up, let them leave a message; this will send a message to your spouse that they are important to you. In order to effectively communicate, you need to be able to express your thoughts and feelings so that it does not put the other person on the defensive. One technique to do this is taking responsibility for your own emotions and your reaction to the issue at hand. For example, I felt hurt when you didn't come home after work, it makes me feel like you take my time for granted. This is very different from you don't care anything about me because you always come home late. Additionally, you want to make sure you don't bombard your partner with information by talking on and on. You should speak in two to three sentences at a time like speaking in bite-sized pieces. If you feel like you have said a mouthful, you have said too much. Speaking in bite-sized pieces gives your mate an opportunity to absorb what you have said and gives them an opportunity to make sure they fully understand the thought that you are trying to convey.

Things to avoid during communication are:

1. Allowing the conversation to escalate. In fact, this can be one of your ground rules in that you will honor one another enough to only speak in love without raising your voice. However, if things do begin to escalate, take time away from each other to calm down and then come back when you can follow through with the conversation from a place of honoring your spouse.
2. Thinking that your spouse can read your mind. You must communicate how you feel in order for him or her to understand how you feel.
3. Don't withdraw, you must also be willing to engage in the conversation even when it may be difficult. It does not help if you withdraw from the conversation, because over time there will be resentment around the issue and towards you because you continue to avoid it.
4. Don't shrug off your spouse's feelings. Accept what your spouse is saying as truth about how they feel. Don't shrug off their feelings as inconsequential or treat them

like, oh here we go again. We must honor each other's feelings without ridicule.

5. Attacking your spouse verbally. You must communicate in a way that your spouse can receive it. Placing demands on your spouse and threatening them in some way does not make them want to communicate with you, it will only push them further away.
6. Name calling
7. Bringing up the past as a support for the argument you are having today especially if your spouse has made real efforts to do better. No one wants to feel like they can't talk to you because what is said will be thrown up in their face later.
8. Stubbornness, the it's my way or the highway mentality.
9. No hitting below the belt and doing things that you know will push your spouse's buttons.

Things to show during communication are:

1. Empathy- showing your spouse or partner that you understand their point of view and see how they feel. For example, your spouse says I get so angry when you don't talk to me about what's going on with you and your plans with your business. It makes me feel like you are trying to hide something. Your response with empathy could be, I see how you could feel that way. I understand how you feel. Another example , your spouse says they are frustrated with you because you have been preoccupied with other things and they have had to carry the load at home. Your response with empathy could be, I can see how you would be frustrated.
2. Validation- by being empathetic to your spouse you can show them that you see their point of view as valid and that you truly have heard what they are saying. An example of validation from the previous scenario is I may have felt like you were trying to hide something

too, if you weren't sharing what was going on with your business. In the second scenario, validation can look like, I would be frustrated too if I had to carry the majority of the load at home for the past 4 months.

Sometimes just empathy and validation can turn around a conversation that may be escalating into an argument. Think about it, what do most couples say in an argument, "if you would just listen to my side you would understand what I'm saying"? Empathy with validation, helps each person feel heard and helps each person feel relieved that, finally, you understand and something truly might be done about your concern.

Does this sound familiar? What if empathy and validation were infused into the picture, you would be showing your spouse that you do hear them and you do understand them, both of which are comforting feelings.

Bible Verses: Proverbs 25:11 *A word fitly spoken is like apples of gold In settings of silver.* **Proverbs 15:23** *A man has joy by the answer of his mouth, And a word spoken in due season, how good it is!*

E- Eliminate Negative Talk (speak the truth in love)

We must speak to each other from a place of honor and of love. Sometimes we can get so bogged down in our negative beliefs about our spouses that we can't see the good in them or the words that they speak. With negative talk and negative thoughts you are putting a negative spin on what your spouse does and says. By doing this, you are allowing the negativity to creep in and distort the words and actions of your spouse. By doing this we put ourselves in the position to feel justified in returning the negative talk or actions. However, we must eliminate the negative talk and thoughts. By eliminating the negative talk we mean the talk that you verbally speak as well as the talk that you have in your head.

According to John Gottman, the respected researcher and psychologist that we told you about in Chapter 1, marriages that are headed for divorce display 4 critical ways of communicating. He calls them the 4 horsemen.

Recognize and avoid the 4 horsemen:

1. Criticism – making comments that attack the other person's character. Ex. You don't know how to cook because you are just too lazy to learn.
2. Defensiveness – this is where you or your spouse takes offense to what is being said and will either fight back or retreat because they feel like they are being wronged by your comments. Ex. I don't have to listen to you because you don't do it either, and what about what you do.
3. Stonewalling – this area is where the person just tunes you out and kind of stares into space until you finish talking. This is a way to soothe themselves to keep from escalating.
4. Contempt – This one is very insidious and very hard to correct because it taints the way you see your spouse. This is where most people are when they are talking about divorce because they have at this stage really grown to dislike their spouse and are angry with them. Ex. I can't stand you. You are so selfish and only think of yourself. I would never be as selfish as you. Only the scum of the earth would treat someone the way you do.

Throughout the book we have given you ways to combat these and show your love for your spouse. The only way to diffuse these is through love, care and concern for your spouse and your relationship, seeing your partner as your spouse and not your enemy.

Bible Verses: Ephesians 5:25-27,29 *Husbands, love your wives, just as Christ also loved the church and gave Himself for her, 26* *that He might sanctify and cleanse her with the washing of water by the word, 27 that He might present her to Himself a glorious church, not having spot or wrinkle or any such thing, but that she should be holy and without blemish. 29 For no one ever hated his own flesh, but nourishes and cherishes it, just as the Lord does the church.*

L – Listen Carefully and Repeat

Just like there is an art to communicating there is an art to listening. When listening to our spouses we must be able to hear what has been said but repeat it back so that we can clarify what they have just said. This is why you only want to speak in bite-sized pieces to not only be fair to yourself but to the listener so that they can correctly repeat back what you have said as they understand it. When listening, you want to give your undivided attention in your nonverbal body language as well as when you repeat back what they have said. Take on an open posture and one the shows that you are interested. In listening carefully, you can't be thinking of whatever your response is or you will have completely missed what is being said. You have to focus totally on what they are saying, not your grocery list or the other things you could be doing with your time. **Bible Verses: Proverbs 18:13, 15** *He who answers a matter before he hears it ,It is folly and shame to him. 15 The heart of the prudent acquires knowledge, And the ear of the wise seeks knowledge.* **James 1:19** *So then, my beloved brethren, let every man be swift to hear, slow to speak, slow to wrath;*

O- Openly Discuss the Problem Involved in the Conflict

This is the time to discuss the problem openly and honestly. This is the time to discuss what the biggest concerns are pertaining to the conflict at hand. During this time, only discuss the issues, don't try to resolve them yet. When discussing the issues, you will employ the effective communication and active listening skills to make sure you are accurately portraying both of your concerns, so that you can come up with the root causes of the issues. Make sure you are only discussing one issue at a time. Many couples find themselves in trouble because they are choosing to discuss multiple issues at a time because they are avoiding them trying to "keep peace". All this does is make the issues grow, build and fester so that when you do start discussing something that you are passionate about all the emotions that you have stuffed for the last year explode and your spouse has no idea where any of this is coming from because you never told them how you felt or if you did you didn't let them know that this particular issue meant that much to you. Openly discussing means that both people get to talk about the issue at hand without backlash or feeling like they have to walk on eggshells. Most people go into relationships not knowing how to deal with conflict or really resolve the issues they have in their relationship, but that is what this chapter is for to help you with understanding your conflict, communicating effectively about it and then finding ways to really solve your problems.

Many of your concerns or issues in your relationship may come from the list of expectations that you have that may not have been met or if they were met, for whatever reason you were still disappointed. You can use the Problem Solving Circle to discuss issues from finances, to chores, to parenting, dealing with in-laws, and on and on.

After openly talking about the issue and both of you having a chance to understand the other's point of view, you will move to the problem resolution stage. **Bible Verses: Proverbs 12:22** *Lying lips are an abomination to the LORD, But those who deal truthfully are His delight.* **Ephesians 4:29-32** *Let no corrupt word proceed out of your mouth, but what is good for necessary edification, that it may impart grace to the hearers. 30 And do not grieve the Holy Spirit of God, by whom you were sealed for the day of redemption. 31 Let all bitterness, wrath, anger,* *clamor, and evil speaking be put away from you, with all malice. 32 And be kind to one another, tenderhearted, forgiving one another, even as God in Christ forgave you.*

One of the tools we use to help with this is called the Problem Solving Circle. We use this tool to help couples get to the root of their issues and then use the causes or indicators to help them develop a plan on how to solve their issues. In the first circle, we show you an example of how to use it. We've put the issue of lack of sex in the middle of the circle and then all the underlying or causes surrounding it. We do this so that you can both clearly see which issue is on the table and allow both of you to state what you feel the main causes are for the issue. In this diagram there are only 8 spaces to share what you feel are the causes for the issue, but you may feel like you have more. You can just attach a line to the circle and then add the other causes.

Problem Solving Circle

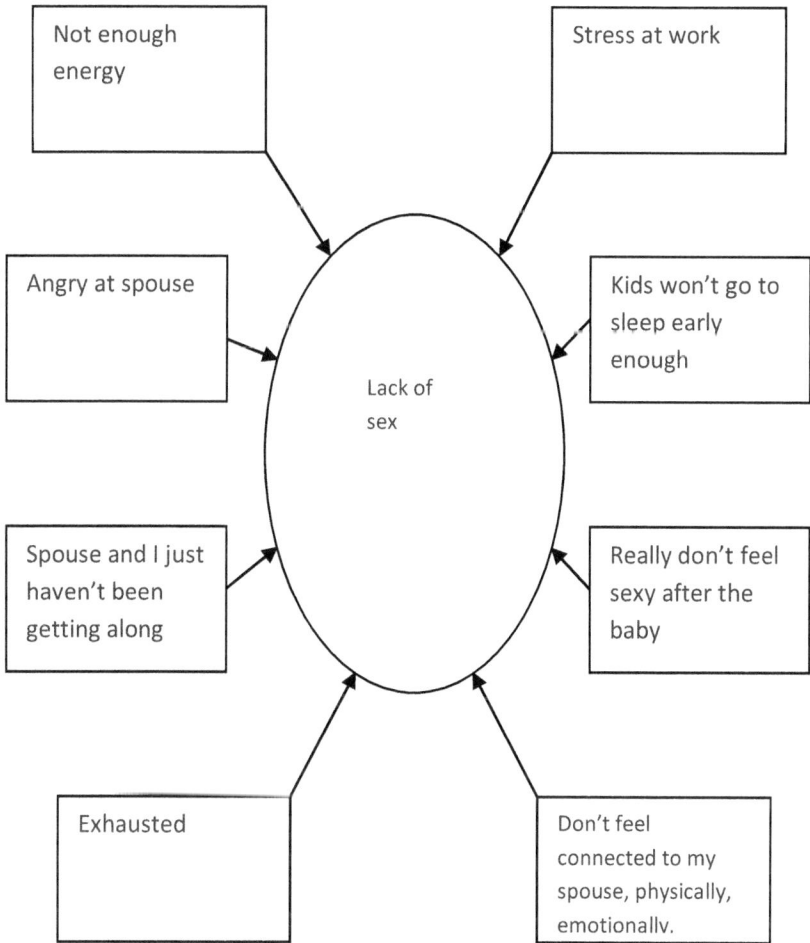

Not enough energy

Stress at work

Angry at spouse

Kids won't go to sleep early enough

Lack of sex

Spouse and I just haven't been getting along

Really don't feel sexy after the baby

Exhausted

Don't feel connected to my spouse, physically, emotionally.

Now in this second circle pick an issue that you have been having with your spouse and place it in the circle. Then in the boxes surrounding the circle, place the causes or indicators of your issue with your spouse.

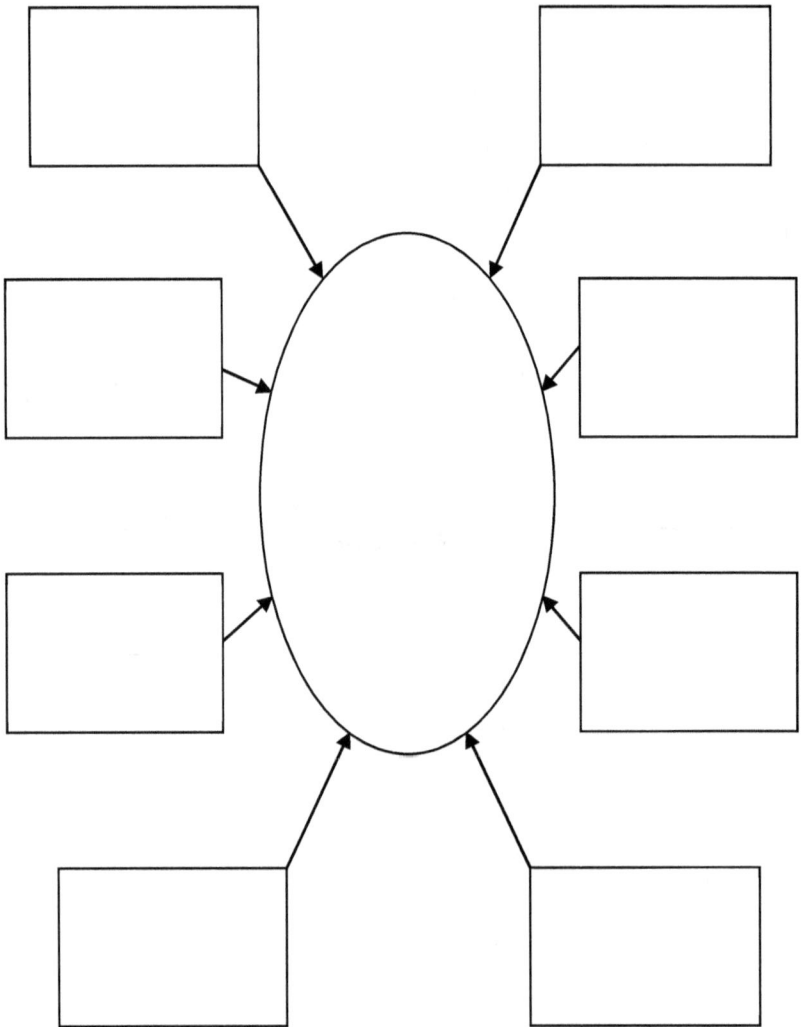

Problem Solving Circle

After you have completed your problem solving circle, pick the top three issues that you feel affect the issue in the middle and put them in rank order from 1 – 3 with 1 being the most important and 3 being the least important. The way to establish which should be number one is to imagine if you dealt with that specific root cause, it could possibly knock out the others or at least affect a great deal of them. In the example, some of the causes could be linked together. There were maybe 3 – 4 categories: 1. Lack of connection 2. Exhaustion 3.Work stress 4. Body Image. If we look at these, the one that could have the most Impact is lack of connection, so they would deal with this one first.

After establishing this, the couple would then come up with a plan to re-establish connection from a physical, emotional and spiritual level in tangible ways. For example, praying together at least 3 times per week, reading the bible together at least 3 times per week, physically touching one another daily during leaving and meeting again, cuddling at night before bed and talking with one another about the day on a daily basis. This may seem simple but it will begin to increase the connection and create something to build on. Later, after you follow up, you can add in dates, sexual contact, whatever you both agree will help rebuild the connection. If rebuilding the connection, was not the number one cause the main issue will not get better, the person won't feel like much progress is being made and you can then go back to the other causes to decide which may be a better fit. We're asking you to do this so you can have a practical plan with real strategies to make your relationship better.

Now rank the causes for your main issue here:

1. _____

_____

2. _____

_____

3. _____

_____

V – Vow to Resolve the Issue and Follow Up

This is now the time where the two of you must determine which factor has the biggest impact on the issue at hand. You can do this by selecting the top 3 and then address the one that you both agree is the #1 factor affecting the problem. After doing this, the two of you need to discuss how you will go about dealing with this factor that suits both of you. Now, set a timetable to complete the work so that you can follow up. This element is key so that you can ensure that the resolution is working and if it is not, you can address what is. This element is also key so that neither of you feels like your spouse does not recognize the efforts you have made, which can cause resentment and backtracking. When you follow up, go over your wins as well as your challenges so that you can keep track of what is working and what is not. When you discover something isn't working you can go back to your discussion and choose another element that may be affecting the problem at hand.

When you discover what is working don't forget to celebrate in a way that you both enjoy. In order to come to a resolution that is best for the marriage and not one individual. You must remember that marriage is a covenant before God. In your covenant with God, you have agreed to die to self or selfishness and give way to the two becoming one flesh. **Issues cannot be resolved from a selfish point of view.**

This step helps to eliminate that merry-go-round feeling you have around some topics that seem to keep popping up. That is because there was never a real resolution or compromise in the first place. The resolutions that the two of you develop have to work for the both of you and if they don't you may have to compromise. True compromise, though, doesn't mean just sucking it up but mumbling and complaining under your breath. True compromise is deciding, I will give in on this point and I truly trust that this will be best for us. For some men this is really hard because they want to have their opinion be the last word, but God has given you a help mate for a reason and it is important that you do take influence from her. She is there to help and not to hurt you and she is there to give you perspective. This is a delicate balance, so women can't take advantage of this privilege by trying to assert what they think is best at all times. Compromise is a give and take from both parties and both have to be willing to give and to take to create the delicate balance of compromise.

E – Experience the Power of the Holy Spirit Through Prayer

Prayer changes things. Sometimes we are in prayer to change the other person and in the end we are the one that is convicted and changed. Prayer is one of the greatest tools God has given us to be in connection with Him. We use prayer as communication with God. Our prayers are also petitions for the health and success of our marriage. In your prayers you should pray from an unselfish standpoint and for the overall benefit of your marriage. Pray prior to entering into the discussion to allow the Holy Spirit to take over. Pray for your anger and other emotions to be under control when speaking to your spouse so that you can convey what it is that you are feeling. Pray that you have an open mind to hear what your spouse is saying from their heart and remove any negative filters or distractions that may get in the way. Pray with confidence that He hears us and that our prayer is according to His will. **Bible Verses: 1 John 5:14-15** *14 Now this is the confidence that we have in Him, that if we ask anything according to His will, He hears us. 15 And if we know that He hears us, whatever we ask, we know that we have the petitions that we have asked of Him.*

Ultimately, when engaging in conflict with your spouse, do it from a place of unselfish love and watch the results of the fruit of your labor. Couples who learn to do this have better relationships because they are able to trust that when issues arise they will be able to discuss them without the rails falling off of their relationship. This type of trust and going through issues but being able to resolve them leads to a greater form of intimacy and a better way to relate to one another. The level of trust and intimacy brought about through being able to go through issues and resolve them makes couples closer because they know that they can depend on one another and it creates a new found sense of connection. So view the issues and conflict in your relationship as a way to get closer to your spouse. The issues that you face may not be unique, but they will be unique to your relationship and if you choose to go through them together in a supportive way, they can bring you closer together and closer to becoming one.

Application Questions:

1. How will you and your spouse change the way you communicate?

2. What areas of communication do you need to change?

3. Where can you take responsibility for the growth of your communication with your spouse?

4. When will you start to make the necessary changes so that you and your spouse can improve your communication?

Be Willing to:

1. Openly discuss issues from a place of love.
2. Accept responsibility for the role you play in your conflict.
3. Show your apology when you are wrong.
4. Make sure that your communication with your spouse is sacred and free from name calling, anger, deceit,

belittlement and any other negative emotion that could create a path to contempt.

5. Pray about your issues with and for your spouse

Ask God:

To bridle your tongue when necessary and give you the words to speak in a manner that your spouse can receive it. Ask God to soften the heart of your mate and allow them to hear you from your heart and not their emotions. Pray for peace throughout your conversation and resolution to the issue at hand.

CHAPTER TWELVE

What's on the Menu, Affection or Rejection?

On a scale of 1-10, how satisfied are you with your sex life? When was the last time you and your spouse communicated sexually? Were you pleased during that time? Was your spouse pleased during your last sexual encounter? Do you feel the way you communicate sexually expresses how you really feel about your spouse?

This chapter is a little bit different from the others because there are so many angles we could have chosen to write from because sex is influenced by so many factors. Because of this, we could have written so much more. This chapter could be a book in and of itself. Either way we tried to keep in line with the book and let sex be just another expression of love that can help you and your spouse divorceproof your marriage. We will however challenge you to see your role in what is or is not working in your sex life and those things you can do differently.

Sex is one of those areas that everyone thinks about (in a positive or a negative way). This area is highly affected by our beliefs formed from our upbringing as well as our own sexual encounters, if any. The area of sex can be a controversial one because so many people have perverted the act of sex, although, it has been designed by God. Because sex involves not only the physical act as well as an emotional and spiritual connection, many factors play a role in the sexual lives of married couples.

Many couples are affected in their bedrooms by decisions that are made in other areas of their lives. We would like you to get to the point of viewing sex as a form of communication between husband and wife rather than a duty that has to be performed. When you view something as a duty that has to be performed there is not much enjoyment to it and therefore you don't want to participate in something that often that you don't look forward to.

Sex is an act of expression, an act of love for one another that is intended for the husband and wife to enjoy. Sex is intended to be the outward expression of your love and commitment for one another. Sex is also the area in the marriage that feels the most attack from the daily trials of life. In I Corinthians 7:1-9 the bible talks about a husband giving himself to his wife and likewise a wife giving herself to her husband on a regular basis as not to give any room for the devil to enter in. Have you noticed that when you and your spouse don't communicate sexually on a regular basis there can be an underlying tension between the two of you? Have you noticed that when you do finally engage in physical communication the walls seem to fall down between the two of you and that ebb and flow that was there before just seems to find its way back?

That is because sex, the act of being physically intimate is a part of God's design for the two to become one flesh. This is the way that God designed for couples to push out the outside world, outside influences and become one, emotionally, spiritually, and physically. Sex is an act designed by God and not shunned by God when it is done within the confines of marriage with your spouse.

How Does Sex Help You Become One?

Becoming one is a part of God's plan for marriage, becoming one in all areas. Oneness in a marriage is partly achieved by having a sexual connection with your spouse. Through sex, you and your spouse are connecting, physically, emotionally, and spiritually. You are physically connecting and one of the hormones that is secreted is Oxyticin, which acts as a bonding agent between you and your spouse. It helps the two of you feel closer after having sex with one another. Connecting emotionally comes when you feel close to your spouse. This area is fostered by having a friendship with your spouse. Spending time together, creating a fun, friendly atmosphere that allows you to trust your spouse and trust that they want to please you and take care of you. You and your spouse connect spiritually by allowing your connection with God to fuel your relationship with your spouse. Allow your intimate relationship with God to help create a more intimate relationship with one another.

Women love to feel like their husbands are leaders in the area of spirituality. They love to feel like their husbands are praying for them, reading and wanting to know more about what God says about being a better man and husband. Women see this as a form of being taken care of by you as the husband because you are seeking God to help you guide your home.

In a similar way, men love to feel like their wives are praying as seeking direction for him as well as your family. They want to feel like you have their best interest at heart. All of this translates into feelings of closeness, intimacy and trust, which allows both men and women to want to be intimate with their spouses. Creating an atmosphere of intimacy helps you want to connect with your spouse regularly and helps you to become one.

What Sex Looks Like to Your Husband

Sex is the way that most men feel physically and emotionally connected to their wives. For men, sex is needed to feel the closeness with his wife and a lack of it could lead to a gap or distance in the relationship. This area can be tricky for women because of the desire to feel close first, but a part of what we are asking you to do is step out of old patterns and create a new way of interacting with one another.

How Does not Having Sex Affect Men

Because sex is such a huge part of the way a man relates to his wife, this area impacts other areas of the marriage in a great way. Ladies, how many times have you turned down your husband when he has approached you for sex? How do you think he feels when this happens? Have you ever thought about it? Turning your husband down has become a part of our culture as something that is widely accepted and not even given a second thought. What if we told you, most men feel rejected when they get turned down? Some men can handle being turned down a few times, maybe even more, but what happens when it appears to be a pattern, where you say no more than you say yes? Do you think your husband would begin to question whether or not you found him attractive or if someone else could be getting your attention? Some of you are thinking that's absurd, how could he think that? Think about it, if your husband turned you down as often as you've turned him down, what would you be thinking? Even if you know your husband well and don't really think these things, is it possible that at times these thoughts would cross your mind? What do you do with those thoughts? Do you let them fester or do you address them? What happens if you do address them? Well, what happened when your husband tried to talk to you about the lack of sex you've been having? How did you respond? Were you understanding and empathetic and made changes? Were you defensive and told him what you needed first so that you could "get in the mood"? Did you tell him that sex was all he thought about, you were tired, you had too much on your plate, tomorrow, I just don't feel like it? How would you feel if these were the responses given to you over and over again? That's exactly how your husband feels.

Rejection for men is a major part of why some men will just stop trying because they just don't want to be rejected anymore, they just don't want their egos shot down anymore. Now we're not trying to make men out to be overly sensitive in this area, but we are trying to bring a different perspective, because sex and whether a couple has it or not is always addressed from the woman's point of view and in a marriage there are two people.

What Sex Looks Like to Your Wife

Sex for women for the most part is highly attached to feeling an intimate connection in order to want to have sex, which is the opposite of what it is for most men. Women want to feel like her husband has thought about her prior to the time they get into the bedroom. Fellas, the way you can show your wife that you are thinking about her prior to that time is by meeting her needs. You learned in Chapter 8 about her needs and which ones she places a high value on. For example, if your wife has a need or places a high value on time spent together, then spend time with her, whether that's during the day over the phone before you get home, watching a movie with her, going out, or just uninterrupted focused attention on her. We know for some this may feel like you have to jump through hoops. Some of you are even saying, man I've done all of this and she still says no, so why even bother, I'll just get it every 6 weeks as usual. When you start to feel this way, remember the ABC's of change in Chapter 3. This is where you have to change your thought about what you think she will do and give her the benefit of the doubt that she is willing and capable of changing. Remember, we are not just asking you to accept your responsibility here, we are also asking your wife to accept her role in the state of your sexual relationship. Meet your wife's needs, create a reciprocal relationship that she can trust that you are not just looking out for yourself here, but that you want to make sure that she is pleased as well.

How the Outside World Impacts Your Relationship

Problem areas in your marriage are reflected in this area of your relationship. If your husband doesn't want to have sex with you, why is that? If your wife doesn't want to have sex with you, why is that? What are they trying to tell you? This is why we say sex is communication because having or not having sex can speak volumes about the state of your relationship. Some outside factors that affect your sex life are children, work, finances, friends, technology, or anything that takes away from the time that you could be spending together or that robs you of your desire to be intimate with your spouse. For example, if you and your spouse are having financial issues it may be hard to want to have sex if you are worried about whether or not the car is going to be repossessed.

What about the ever present existence of children. Parenting can be an exhausting job especially in the early years where you can be sure to include lack of sleep. Many women say at the end of the night after having dealt with their children feeding, bath time, crying, home work, you name it; the last thing on their mind is responding to the advances of their husband. Both are entitled to their feelings in these scenarios but you have to ask yourself what damage are you doing to your relationship when there are more days that you have said no or are not having sex than there are of you saying yes and enjoying each other physically. There are remedies to any situation that is affecting your sex life, but both parties have to be willing to do their part to make this happen. Sex takes planning and work especially if children are involved.

When we work with couples in premarital counseling undoubtedly we'll get a couple who will say they don't want to schedule sex, that takes away from the intimacy or they don't want to think of it as work and they will be having sex 4 or 5 times a week. (Mind you this happens before they have kids, financial problems, loss of jobs, an abundance of conflict ... you name it.) Fast forward two years later after life, children and other things have entered the bedroom and they are not having sex those 4 or five times a week, they are barely having it once a week. They now have to be more planned than spontaneous and someone in the relationship is angry, frustrated and may even be seeking out attention elsewhere. Can you relate to any part of this scenario? Have you related at any point in your relationship? Do you wish you couldn't relate?

Hindrances to a Passionate Sex Life (Things to Avoid)

1. Outside issues/ stressors (work, money, children)

2. Thoughts/ ideas about sex

3. Past trauma (if trauma has never been dealt with professional help may be necessary)

4. Poor past sexual encounters

5. Images of others or involvement with others (i.e.: magazines, phone or internet sex with others, pornography, internet/ social media relationships with others Facebook, Twitter, Instagram, E-mail)

6. Physical or medical issues

7. Poor body image

8. Fear of pregnancy

9. Infertility

10. Low sex drive

11. Pain during sex

12. Infidelity- whether this is physical infidelity or emotional infidelity. Physical infidelity is when you are having sex with someone outside of your marriage, and there may or may not be a relationship with this outside person. Emotional infidelity is when you are having an emotional affair with someone where you share your inner most thoughts and feelings; things that you would normally share with your spouse, but have chosen instead to share with someone else. Emotional infidelity feels more like a relationship and you are spending time, feelings and attention with someone other than your spouse. Infidelity that involves both the physical and emotional element can be the most toxic and the hardest to end because a bond has been formed both physically and emotionally.

Things to avoid that may be affecting your relationship:

1. Criticism of your spouse in and out of the bedroom

2. Resentment of your spouse

3. Anger towards your spouse

4. Waiting only for the sexual act to show love

5. Infidelity

How to Have a Passionate / Fun Sex Life

In the previous section, we discussed how outside factors and hindrances can affect your sexual relationship. In this section, we want to help you understand how you and your spouse can have a more passionate and intimate relationship.

1. **Shamelessness**- This element is important especially in the American culture because of all of the messages that we are given about sex. Some images are that sex is not something that should be talked about in public let alone to have questions asked about it. Even though our society has changed a lot, parents are still not the primary source of sex education for their children. Because the education we have received around sex comes from a varied amount of places including a predominance of distorted images, it is hard not to include what we have or have not learned into our sexual relationship with our spouse.

   Unfortunately, this is also one of those tricky areas where many people have experienced some sort of bad sexual experience from molestation to a bad relationship and may have some shame about their body or even the act of sex itself. Because of this, it is important that you and your spouse openly talk about any sexual experiences that you may have had in the past so that you both can be aware of how this may affect your current sexual relationship. This is a very sensitive area and will need to be handled delicately.

   Sex is such an intimate act of giving of oneself to the other that a lot of trust is involved especially for women and it can be hard to get past some issues that may have occurred in the past. Working through any issues can help alleviate any shame that may be plaguing your sex life so that the two of you can enjoy one another without any shame or embarrassment getting in the way of the two of you fully enjoying the pleasure of indulging in one another. An example that can help alleviate the shame is lying naked with your spouse and exploring one another's bodies in a way that both of you feel comfortable.

2. **Selflessness**- This is a big one in relationships. Many people complain that they don't enjoy their sex life because they are not being pleased and only the partner seems to be getting something out of it. You can't be a selfish lover and expect that your spouse will want to continue to engage in sex with you on a regular basis. How long would you participate in something if you rarely, if ever got anything out of it? We would dare to say, not long. Here again is why we say communication is so key when dealing with sex. You have to communicate with one another about what you like, don't like, what you want and don't want. Don't go into the relationship trying to please your spouse based on what you and your last partner used to do. Get to know what the two of you like and make sure you work to please one another each time you meet up sexually. If you are both working to please the other, you will both be pleased every time. Create an atmosphere where the two of you desire one another full of raw passion. Sex is an area where disappointment and resentment can be built up fast if your partner feels like you're the only one working to "get your rocks off".

3. **Communication**- Okay this is probably one of **THE** most important elements to a satisfying sex life. How do you know what your partner likes or dislikes if you don't talk about it? How do you know if what they like has changed because as we grow and change so do some of our likes and dislikes? When was the last time you asked your spouse, does what I do for you sexually please you? When was the last time you and your spouse talked about sex at all? Sex can be one of those areas in your relationship that you just do without putting much thought into it, just like money, which is why these two are the primary reasons that people get divorced. You have to communicate about sex to find out if your partner enjoys it to see if there are any issues inhibiting your sex life, if there are any medical issues that are plaguing this area, any taboos, past relationships, sexual trauma. Communicate, communicate, communicate. I know some of you men are saying, dang; you really want me to talk about this area too. Don't we already talk enough, this is just one other thing. I thought I was already good in this area. Brothers, I promise you getting in tune with your wife in this area can make for a more satisfying experience for her, which will make it more satisfying for you. Just try it.

4. **Serving or Giving** - Cater to your spouse. When was the last time you catered to your spouse in the bedroom? Serve your spouse in a way that they are the center of your attention and affection. Please them in the way that they like and focus less on your needs. Your sole desire here is to make sure that they are happy and are enjoying themselves. Doing so can prove to be equally

as pleasurable for you. It can create a reciprocal effect where you please them, they please you, and it continues to go around and around. What are the things that your spouse has asked you to do over and over again but you just haven't tried it? Maybe you haven't because that part of your life is sort of routine and you're in a rut and you just tell yourself, ah, I just don't feel like it or that will take too much effort. Let's just get it over with. You want this to be an area that you both look forward to and enjoy it when you do get together so you want to come back for more on a regular basis. Give your spouse a sensual massage where the two of you are naked. Please them in all the ways they have been asking for and then the next night, have your spouse please you. Create reciprocity where you both feel like no one else matters when the two of you are together.

5. **Consistency** – Consistency is key. It is important that you communicate sexually on a regular basis. Lack of communication sexually can cause you to get into a rut and the longer you don't engage in any sexual activity, the easier it will become to just become roommates and become a part of the alarming statistics of having a sexless marriage. A sexless marriage is one in which you and your partner only have sex 10 or less times per year. If this is something you have already fallen into, you and your spouse need to survey what has happened to that part of your relationship and work to fix it.

6. **Friendship** – Creating an atmosphere of friendship, playfulness and appreciation for one another physically emotionally and spiritually. Take the time to flirt with

one another even when others are around to heighten the desire for one another. Lay with each other in the nude and learn to appreciate and enjoy all parts of your spouse's body. Create a code word that only the two of you know means sex, so that when you are out, or in front of others you can use the code word to signal to your spouse that you are ready to be intimate with one another when you have a chance.

7. **Prayer**- I know some of you are thinking, now where did that come from, but God is concerned about all areas of your life, including your sex life with your spouse. Pray for your sex life just like you would any other aspect of your life. Allow this to enhance the spiritual and intimate connection that you and your spouse have together. Pray before you two have sex and see how intense the experience can become.

How Do You Get Your Mojo Back After It Has Been Lost?

1. Make sure there are no medical reasons that the two of you are not having sex. Go get a physical to ensure there are no physical concerns.
2. Make sure there are no other issues impeding your desire to want to have sex. Women have a tendency in the work we have done to let other issues that bother them impede the sex process. So if they are angry or hurt about something, the women find it hard to have sex with their husband. Talk about your concerns.
3. Make sure you are not using the lack of sex as a punishment. Sex is not a weapon. You cannot use sex as a way to keep your spouse in line. Sex as God designed it is a part of His plan to make the two one. In fact in 1Corinthians 7:5, the bible states "do not deprive one another except with consent for a time that you may

give yourselves to fasting and prayer; and come together again so that Satan does not tempt you because of your lack of self-control". Depriving one another creates a gap in the space where the two are to become one which leaves room for other things and other people to come in and fill that void.

NOTE: We have had so many couples come to us for help due to infidelity because they have not been providing for each other's sexual needs among others. Sex is an important part of a marriage to help the two of you become one.

4. Talk about whatever issues may be blocking you from having sex with one another. Talk about whether or not you find your sexual time together pleasurable. Be willing to make some changes if necessary.
5. Create the atmosphere for intimacy in your relationship. It's hard to go from no sex for some time to desiring to be with one another every night. Create the space where you are meeting each other's needs and acting on them. Meeting your spouse's needs can really turn things around.
6. When your spouse approaches you let there be more times of acceptance and love versus the amount of times you turn them away or reject them.
7. Create intimate moments where there is no sexual act intended, but the two of you are touching one another, kissing and caressing. This will help with the build up to the actual sexual act.
8. Make time to have sex with one another. Incorporate meeting one another's needs throughout the day, being loving and intimate throughout the day and then commit to being sexually intimate that night.
9. Make a commitment to have more sex on a regular basis because the more sex you have, if both are pleased, the more sex you want to have. Our bodies

create a hormone called oxytocin which acts like a bonding agent when we are intimate. Have you ever noticed that you feel closer to your spouse after you have sex with one another?

10. Remove any obstacles to the two of you having sex. Stop viewing images of other men or women, stop using pornography or any outside images that take away from your spouse being the center of attention sexually. You two may not be having as much sex or it may not be as pleasurable, because one or both of you have found another way to be pleased. Allow your spouse to be the only form of stimulation you use so that they can be the focus of your physical affection.

Incorporate these tips to help improve and increase your sex life. When it appears you have gotten into a rut, follow these tips again to get out of it. Overall, make a commitment to fulfill each other's needs out of the bedroom so there will be no issues when it comes time to fulfill each other's needs in the bedroom.

Sex in marriage is one of God's gifts to marriage. Learn how to please your spouse and allow your spouse to please you.

Application Questions:

1. Are there any issues in your past that you need to address that may be affecting your sexual relationship with your spouse?

2. Is there anything physically wrong with you that may be affecting your relationship with your spouse? If so, how do you plan to address it?

3. How will you improve the way that you please your spouse?

4. How can you show your spouse that this area is important to you and that you want to make sure they are pleased in the process?

5. What's your plan for making and maintaining sex as a priority in your marriage?

6. What can you do to make your sex life the complete physical, emotional and spiritual experience with your spouse?

7. If you have taken your spouse for granted or caused any rejection, what can you do differently to make your spouse feel wanted and appreciated?

Be Willing to:

1. Look at what you can do to improve your sexual relationship.

2. Remove anything that may be a hindrance to your sexual intimacy with your spouse.

3. Fulfill your spouse's needs before your own.

4. Create an atmosphere of intimacy through physical, emotional and spiritual connection.

5. Seek outside help if needed to address any past or present issues.

6. Be honest with your spouse about this area of your marriage and what you are willing to do to make it better and what you would like them to do to make it better.

7. Invite God into your bedroom.

Ask God:

To help reveal any issues that may be standing in the way of the two of you becoming one. To help remove any barriers you have to being intimate with your spouse on a regular basis. To provide the desire, energy and connection needed to create the sexual experience you both desire. To create a sexual relationship that allows you both to fulfill the others needs each time you meet and that this part of your relationship is pleasing to God.

CHAPTER THIRTEEN

Without a Vision, Your Marriage will Perish

What role does spirituality play in your marriage? Do you believe that God plays an integral role in your relationship? Have you incorporated prayer into your relationship? Do you believe that prayer can change things in your relationship? Does prayer play a role in the way you communicate, parent your children, operate daily in your marriage, your sex life with your spouse? Many books that deal with marriage shun away from dealing with spirituality as a part of the marital relationship. We chose to address it head on because we believe that your relationship with God plays a significant role in your marital relationship. In fact, we believe that God's role in your relationship is the glue that holds the two of you together and without Him, it is much harder to make the relationship work. Because we believe that in a marriage the couple is striving to become one with their spouse, but there are so many obstacles, the help of someone greater than you is needed to make the marriage work. We believe that in our own will or strength, there will be times that you just won't be able to move forward. In every aspect of your relationship, God needs to be a part. He is able to give you that peace that you need even when you don't desire to have it. What about those times that the two of you have had an argument and you really want to give your spouse a couple of words that you know you wouldn't say to your boss, pray in that moment. Ask God to hold your tongue, give you the words to speak and to soften the heart of your spouse so that they are ready to receive it. Have you ever done this or were you so angry that you didn't even think of this? You can incorporate God into all aspects of your marriage through prayer, devotion, and scripture.

Through prayer, you can pray specifically for your spouse, yourself and your marriage. The prayer for your spouse has to come from an unselfish place, however, even if it doesn't, God will convict you. What we mean by this is you can't pray, God please change my spouse so they can see my side, so they will do what I want; you get the point. Your prayer for your spouse has to be an unselfish one that really is for their betterment and in turn will make your relationship better. For example, God please bless my husband to understand what you would have him to be as a father to our children and that he is more like you as a father. Prayer is just an ongoing conversation between you and God. God is your friend and he wants to hear from you like a friend. He's concerned about every area of your life and wants the best for you.

Devotion can be an opportunity and time for you and your spouse to read a daily devotion together that is specifically geared to married couples. These are small passages that give you advice based on scripture on a daily basis. This is one way for you and your spouse to start or end your day on the same page. You can also incorporate a daily devotion that you have just for yourself and your relationship with God.

Finally, you and your spouse can read scripture together and talk about what God is telling you in the scripture. You can choose scripture that is specifically geared to marriage and or to a specific issue that you are having. The bible is really meant to be a guidebook for everyday life and used as a way to govern your life.

Many people are leary of this area either because of what they've seen or haven't seen and may not know how to incorporate spirituality into their everyday life. Ultimately, it all boils down to relationship, having a relationship with God and spending time with him. The bible speaks of abiding in God, which means having God live inside of you, but the only way this can happen is by spending time with him. Spending time with God through prayer, devotion, reading the bible and praise and worship. Worshipping God is just a way of showing God how much you love and care about him. This is where you are completely focused on him and not on what your needs are. Spending time with him allows you to build a better relationship just like you would with your spouse. How else do you get to know someone unless you spend time with them?

At first spending time with God may seem a little weird or a little robotic, but we believe that the time spent will allow you to get to know him better, because he already knows you. He created you. He loves you! He loves you when no one else loves you. He is the one that you should pattern your love for your spouse after. His love supersedes all others and if you have never seen this love in the flesh before, your spouse is the one who should be able to show it to you. This type of relationship just like anything else takes work, time and commitment. Just like any other relationship, there will be times where you will feel distant and not necessarily wanting to spend time. In those times, you will feel a tugging or small little twinge like something is missing. If the distance becomes even further, you may feel a slightly harder tug to get your attention. If you ignore that one, then the tug becomes a little harder and you may be set still.

Have you ever had a time where you were just moving constantly and you felt like your life was on fast forward, from work, spouse, family, home, your civic group, fraternity or sorority and maybe even church and because of this it has been days, weeks or even months since the last time that you really sat down and talked to God? At those times, God may allow you to get that bug that has been going around, but instead of slightly making you sick, like everyone else, it knocks you out. You have to take some time off work, that group, from church. You have to be still. When it is still and quiet, what do you do? You think. In those quiet moments is when you can hear from God clearly. He speaks to us through our spirit and tells us what he wants us to hear and what direction he would have for us to go. If we are never still, if you never make time for him, how do you think he should get your attention? Spend time with God, give him the attention he needs, the love he needs, abide in him. In John 15:7 Jesus says abide in me and I in you and ask whatever you wish according to my will and it shall be given. Spending time with God gives you the opportunity to get to know him better and to know what his will is for your life, so your prayers to him are in line with what he would have you to do in your life. The better you know him the better you will be at making sure you line up with what he wants from you.

Your relationship with God and allowing him to be the glue of your relationship with your spouse will set your marriage apart from others. Others will wonder why it seems like the two of you seem to love each other so much and that your spouse seems to reverence you and treat you with so much love and respect. Others will desire to have what you have. Ultimately, the truth about marriage is God. God is the truth about marriage, because God is love. He is agape love, the kind of love that loves regardless of your flaws, appreciates you for who you are, forgives you when you wrong, speaks to you in a loving way, wants to meet your needs as a human and even further as an individual, he wants to know you better than anyone else. He loves you no matter what baggage you bring to the table. In fact, your flaws are what make him love you even more because those same faults are what he can use to show others that he loves the flawed. These same flaws are what shows others, through your transparency, that you too are human, you too have made mistakes, and you too are loved regardless of them. Your relationship will then be an advertisement for God it will show others what his love looks like in the flesh. Your relationship if done in this way can show others how Christ loves the church. Your relationship shows how he loves and protects her, reverences her and would lay down his life for her and even died for her. With all that we do, we want to make sure you get the practical application as to how this works.

What does reverencing your spouse look like? What does protecting and providing look like? What does dying for your spouse look like? We know that dying part sounds a little deep, but what we mean by that is allowing those things in you and certain behaviors to die so that you can be a better image of what Christ would have you to be as a person as well as a wife or husband. So if your yelling, nagging, cussing, cheating, poor money management doesn't look like God, then those things will be pruned or cut away from you so that you can be more like him. Going through the process of pruning helps you become more like Christ so that others can recognize his traits in you.

A marriage is one of the greatest discipling moments. We are usually the closest person to our spouse so we see most if not all of their flaws and those things that are not like God. We can encourage our spouses to make the changes needed to be more like Christ, but in a loving way. We can pray that they become more like Christ and then we can display what it looks like as well. Learning from an example, teaching, relationship and prayer is discipleship.

SPIRITUALITY / VISION

We believe above all other issues we discussed here; the spiritual connection you share will by far allow you to have the relationship you desire. No one in their own strength can love a person full of flaws unconditionally for a lifetime. It is imperative that you learn what you both think about spirituality and the role that it plays in your family's future. It is also vitally important that you develop a plan or a vision for your family so that you don't get thrown off by the ups and downs of life. Please answer the following questions to help you understand your thoughts on spirituality as well as your spouse.

1. What vision or plan do you have for your family?

   _____
   _____
   _____
   _____
   _____
   _____
   _____

2. Do you and your spouse agree on how spirituality impacts your family and children? Please explain.

   _____

_____

_____

_____

_____

_____

3. Do you and your spouse agree about religious values
    and beliefs? If not, is that a problem? Please explain.

_____

_____

_____

_____

4. Do you and your spouse agree on what church you will
    attend, the frequency of attendance and involvement in
    church?

_____

_____

_____

_____

_____

_____

_____

5. Do you and your partner pray together?

_____

6. Are you satisfied with the amount of prayer time the
    two of you share? If not, what do you believe this
    should look like?

_____

_____

_____

_____

_____

_____

7. Do you and your spouse read the bible or do devotions together? If not, what do you believe this should look like?

_____

_____

_____

_____

_____

_____

_____

8. **Overall**, how satisfied are you in your spiritual relationship with your mate?

   1) extremely **un**satisfied
   2) moderately **un**satisfied
   3) slightly **un**satisfied
   4) slightly satisfied
   5) moderately satisfied
   6) extremely satisfied

9. **Overall**, how satisfactory do you think your spiritual relationship is to your mate?

   1) extremely **un**satisfactory
   2) moderately **un**satisfactory
   3) slightly **un**satisfactory
   4) slightly satisfactory
   5) moderately satisfactory
   6) extremely satisfactory

10. Are there any barriers to your spiritual life with your spouse? If so, what are they?

_____

_____

_____

_____

_____

_____

_____

11. What are your expectations of your spouse and how
    your spiritual life should look together?

_____

_____

_____

_____

_____

_____

_____

_____

12. Do you feel like you and your spouse are moving
    forward, stalled or moving backwards in your spiritual
    life together?

_____

_____

_____

_____

_____

_____

13. How do you feel about this?

_____

_____

_____

_____

_____

_____

This area of your relationship will help you want to
maintain your friendship, will hold you accountable to love your

spouse the way Christ loves you, to forgive your spouse even when you know you don't want to. Your spiritual connection will increase your desire for your spouse when everyone else around you is talking about divorce. Spirituality is also the area that allows you to see the true growth of your spouse. It helps you disciple your spouse into the image of Christ from a place of love. We see marriage as the greatest discipleship moment there is.

Vision and spirituality go hand in hand because in order to move forward even in your spiritual life, you must have a vision. Everyone has a vision of what they think their life should look like, even if you may not have written it down. So let's start now.

1. What's your vision for your family? (The overall long term goal for your family)

_____

_____

_____

_____

_____

_____

_____

_____

2. What's the mission for your family? (The idea or values that govern your family)

_____

_____

_____

_____

_____

_____

_____

_____

3. What are some of the scriptures you can use to guide your family?

_____

_____

_____

_____

_____

_____

4. Based on the work you've done in the book, what is the long-term goal for your family that you want to have accomplished by this time next year? (Use the work you did to assess your relationship in Chapter 2, the expectations and values in Chapter 8 and the issues addressed in the problem-solving section in the communication chapter to help you find the overall goal for the year. The goal for the year should reflect what issue you and your spouse see as the number one concern for the forward growth of your relationship and if you addressed that issue in your relationship, many other issues would be handled.)

_____

_____

_____

_____

_____

_____

_____

_____

_____

_____

Under the goal for the year, you should set intermediate goals. Intermediate goals are smaller goals that will help you accomplish your overall goal for the year. Use the work you did in previous chapters to help you develop the intermediate goals. Under each intermediate goal, you will set even smaller incremental goals or objectives that can be accomplished in shorter periods of time from a week to a month.

5. What are some smaller intermediate goals and objectives that you can set to help you reach your overall goal for the year?

These goals should help you accomplish your overall goal and should have a time limit as well. Keep them simple and something that you both agree can be carried out. For example, if your overall goal was to improve your communication so that by this time next year, you two can communicate in a way that honors the other with no forms of disrespect and you will have only argued twice throughout the year. (Honor and disrespect were defined by you when you discussed setting a safe place to talk under the AGAPE LOVE model in the communication chapter)

One intermediate or smaller goal could be, we will communicate weekly without any cursing, yelling or name calling. The goal here is to communicate weekly and the sub-goals are to eliminate the cursing, yelling or name calling. Another goal could be, if we start to see our communication turning into an argument, we will do a. b. c. to turn the situation around. By giving yourself a plan and a way to execute it, you are providing a blueprint for your success.

1) _____
   _____
   _____
   _____
   _____
   _____

a. _____
_____
_____
_____
_____

b. _____
_____
_____
_____
_____

c. _____
_____
_____
_____
_____
_____

2) _____
_____
_____
_____
_____

a. _____
_____
_____
_____

b. _____
_____
_____
_____

c. _____
   _____
   _____
   _____
   _____
   _____
   _____

3) _____
   _____
   _____
   _____
   _____
   _____

a. _____
   _____
   _____
   _____
   _____

b. _____
   _____
   _____
   _____

c. _____
   _____
   _____
   _____

One of the biggest complaints we get in sessions is that we keep arguing about the same things and we never come to a conclusion. If you develop a plan of action and then follow up, you can see where you have gone backwards, moved forward or stalled. Use your plan as a blueprint in conjunction with biblical principles to help guide you and your relationship in the right direction.

Now that you've learned all of this, what are your next steps?

After completing your plan, create a vision board, a visual reminder of what you want in your relationship. We would love to see your plans as well as your vision boards, so we want you to email us at alisha@themarriagecoaches.net a picture of your vision board and a copy of your plan within the next 30 days. If you do this, we will send you a coupon good for a discount for one of our upcoming events, valid for 1 year. We can't wait to see and hear your progress. God is able to do all things!

Application Question:

1.   When will you and your spouse get started on your vision and plan for your marriage?

2.   What can you do to make sure God is the glue that holds your relationship together?

3.   What do you see as something that can hinder the success of your plan?

4.   What can you do to head off the hindrances before they take hold of the progress you have made?

5.   What ways can you hold yourself accountable to continue to move forward to make your relationship look like what you desire it to be?

6. How can you and your spouse work together to make this happen?

7. How will your marriage be different from this point forward?

Be Wiling:

1. To pray for your spouse on a regular and consistent basis.
2. To set a new goal and vision for your marriage if your old one isn't working.
3. To incorporate God into all aspects of your marriage and allow him to navigate the relationship.

Ask God:

To create the relationship he would like for you and your spouse to have. To convict you when you are wrong. To show you how to truly love, nourish and care for your spouse. To allow your relationship to become a light in darkness and be a blessing to someone else who may be struggling to see that they can love being married.

CHALLENGE TO JOIN THE I LOVE BEING MARRIED MOVEMENT

CHAPTER FOURTEEN

Get Out of the Boat

Well you've come to the end of our book. We really do appreciate you taking the time to read the book, but now what? We don't want you to read this book and allow it to collect dust. We want you to read this book and take action. You can take action by doing the exercises in the book and having your spouse do them as well. If your spouse isn't interested in the book or the activities, then you do them on your own and lead the way. Let them see the changes in you regardless of what they do or don't do. Let your spouse see that you want the relationship to work no matter what. If your marriage is already in a good place then allow this book and the activities in it to make your relationship better.

What have you gained by reading this book? Have you already seen some changes in your relationship? Were the changes for the better? At the beginning of the book, you rated what you felt your relationship was like on a scale of 1 -10, what do you think now? If the number has improved, what has changed to make the relationship better? If the number is the same or lower, what can you do differently to make the number improve, if only a half point? Remember a big part of what we teach and believe is that you need to take responsibility for your role in whatever is right or wrong with your relationship, even if the only wrong that you have done is not speak up for yourself.

As we stated earlier in the book we want to encourage more couples to be able to say and mean it when they say, I Love Being Married! This statement is not an easy one to make, nor is it one that you will feel at all times, but it can be a goal that you aspire to. In having this be the mantra for your marriage, you can encourage yourself in the bad times and keep you on the positive side when things are going well. You can post it in your bedroom, on your bathroom mirror, on the refrigerator, in your car, anywhere that will serve as a reminder of the goal that you are trying to reach or maintain. You can create a vision board with all of the images and sayings that you feel will help you and your spouse keep the idea of loving being married. When making the vision board for your marriage, the two of you should be involved, however as we stated before some spouses will not want to be a part and that is when you do it by yourself and put it in a prominent place so that your spouse can see as well.

By reading this book, you and your spouse are on your way to a better marriage whatever place you are in. You are now among the number of people who are pledging to change the direction of marriage and the perception of marriage. We challenge you to use this book over and over again as a tool to make your marriage better year after year. We've called this chapter, Get Out of the Boat because there is a time in the bible in Matthew 14:22-33 where Peter, one of Jesus' disciples had to learn to trust God even in the midst of his storm. God was calling to him to get out of the boat and trust that he would keep him afloat as he walked on water even though there were rough winds swirling around the boat. Well, we're calling to you to get out of the boat even with the struggles, pain, issues, craziness that may be swirling around in your life and trust God with your relationship. In doing so, we are calling you to action to improve your relationship and use your story to help someone else. When you focus your attention on others, it helps you see that your problems may not be as bad and others can be inspired by your story.

Whether you're happily married and just want to enhance your marriage, or your marriage has some issues that need to be addressed or you are single and curious about what it takes to love being married, you can join us by:

1. Going to our website www.ilovebeingmarried.net and taking the pledge that we've created to encourage you to Love Being Married.
2. Sharing your story via email, FB post, tweet or video, telling us why you love being married.
3. Emailing us your receipt to orders@ilovebeingmarried.net to get a 30% savings code to register for an I Love Being Married Experience or our 8 week online e-course.
4. Becoming a part of our I Love Being Married Community by starting an I Love Being Married group in your area by using the tools we have on our website.
5. Becoming a part of the I Love Being Married team as an affiliate and helping us promote and sell our book, t-shirts, and events, where you can earn a percentage of your sales.
6. Joining our email list.
7. Joining our Facebook community at The Marriage Coaches and Twitter @iluvbeinmarried using the hashtag #ilovebeingmarried.
8. Having us speak at your event on various relationship topics for married, engaged and single people in all

settings, i.e. community group, mommy group, parent meeting, church, fraternity or sorority.

9. Encouraging someone else to make their marriage better.
10. Praying for your marriage and others.

If you want specific help for your marriage from us, you can contact us via our website so that you can find and select the most appropriate need.

We can't wait to hear from you about how you can now say, I Love Being Married. We are excited to see what God has in store for your marriage!

APPENDIX

Walker Marriage Assessment Tool

Acceptance	Appreciation	Friendship	Love	Forgiveness	Expectations	Trust	Communication	Sex	Spirituality

Criticism	Appreciation

Expectation/ Value/ Need	Rate the importance of the expectation on scale of 1-10	Rate how your spouse is meeting this expectation on a scale of 1-10	I am willing	I am willing but...	I am not willing

Figure 8.1

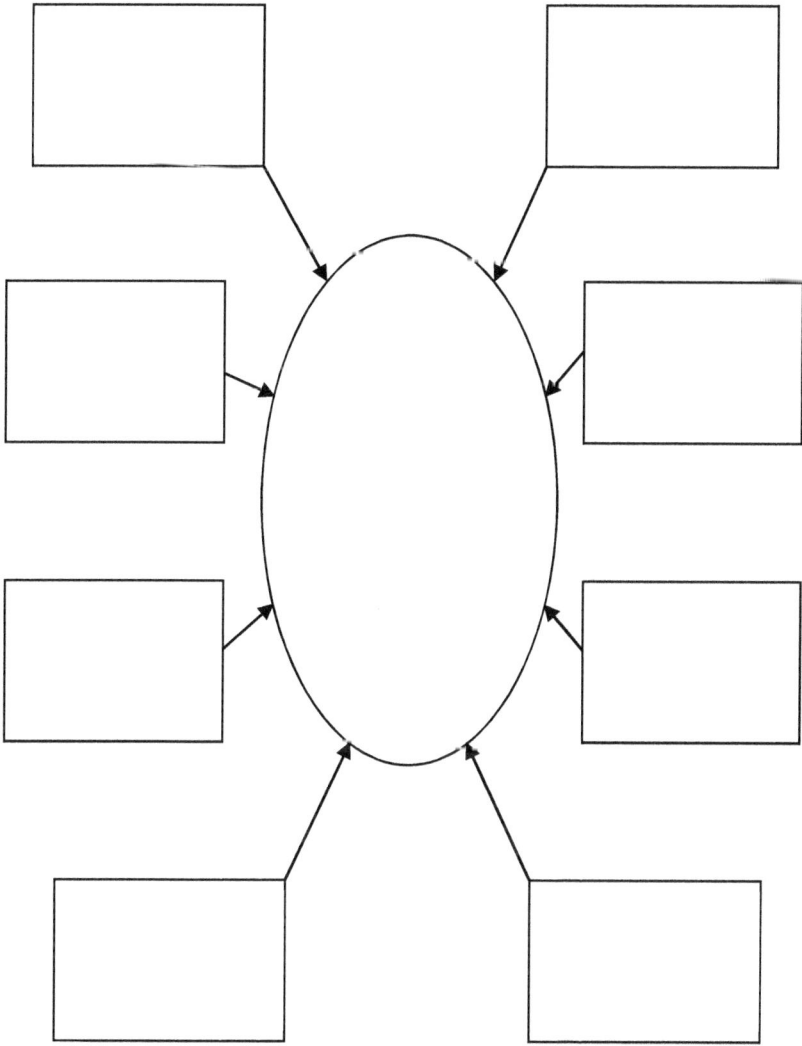

Problem Solving Circle

NOTES

Dr. John Gottman, *Marital Therapy: A Research-Based Approach* (The Gottman Institute, 2000)

Dr. Willard F. Harley, Jr., *His Needs Her Needs: Building an Affair-Proof Marriage* (Grand Rapids: Revell, 1986)

David & Claudia Arp, *10 Great Dates to Energize Your Marriage* (Grand Rapids: Zondervan, 1997)

H. Norman Wright, *After You Say I Do* (Eugene: Harvest House, 1999)

Stephen and Alex Kendrick, *The Love Dare* (Nasville: B&H Publishing Group, 2008)

Kay Arthur, *A Marriage Without Regrets* (Chattanooga: Precept Ministries International, 1981)

Sheila Wray Gregoire, *The Good Girl's Guide to Great Sex* (Grand Rapids: Zondervan, 2012)

Bruce and Toni Hebel, *Forgiving Forward: Unleashing the Forgiveness Revolution* (Regenerating Life Press, 2011)

Dr. Gary Chapman, *The Five Love Languages: The Secret to Love that Lasts* **(Chicago: Northfield, 1992)**

Kay Arthur, *The Truth About Sex: What the World Won't Tell You & God Wants You to Know*(Colorado: WaterBrook, 2002)

Rick Warren, *The Purpose Driven Life: What on Earth am I Here For?* (Grand Rapids: Zondervan, 2003)

Dr. Ed Wheat and Claudia Okes Perkins *Love Life for Every Married Couple: How to Fall in Love, Stay in Love, Rekindle Your Love* (Grand Rapids: Zonderva, 1980)